ON ROYAL AND PAPAL POWER

UNIVERSA PRESS — WETTEREN (BELGIUM)

JOHN OF PARIS

ON ROYAL AND PAPAL POWER

Translated with an Introduction

by

J. A. WATT

THE PONTIFICAL INSTITUTE OF MEDIAEVAL STUDIES
TORONTO, CANADA
1971

Cover drawing adapted from the
Heidelberg ms. (early 14th century)
of the *Sachsenspiegel*.

TABLE OF CONTENTS

PREFACE

As early as the fourteenth century there was interest in England in translating the literature of the controversy between Pope Boniface VIII and Philip IV of France. John Trevisa († c. 1400) sometime Fellow of Queen's College, Oxford, translated the *Dialogus inter militem et clericum,* a tract, like the treatise of John of Paris translated here, written in support of the French king. I have worked in the spirit of Trevisa's approach to the translation of this genre of political writing:

> In some place I shall set word for word and actiffe for actiffe and passife for passife arowe (*i.e.* in order) right as it standeth without changing the order of words. But in some places I must change the order of words and set actiffe for passife and azen word. And in some places I must set a reason for a word and tell what it meaneth; But for all such changing the meaning shall stand and not be changed.[1]

I have made use of three editions of the *De potestate regia et papali*: M. Goldast, *Monarchiae sancti Romani Imperii* (1614) 2. 108-47: J. Leclercq, *Jean de Paris et l'ecclésiologie du XIIIᵉ siècle* (Paris 1942); F. Bleienstein, *Johannes Quidort von Paris Ueber königliche und päpstliche Gewalt. Textkritische Edition mit deutscher Uebersetzung* (Stuttgart 1969). I have consulted translations of different

---

[1] *Trevisa's Dialogue...* ed. J. A. PERRY, *Early English Texts Society* 167 (1925) xxxiv.

extracts from the treatise made by E. Lewis, *Medieval Political Ideas,* 2 vols (New York 1954); J. Leclercq, *L'idée de la royauté du Christ au moyen âge* (Paris 1959); E. T. Fortin in *Medieval Political Philosophy: a Source-book* ed. R. Lerner and M. Mahdi (New York 1963); B. Tierney, *The Crisis of Church and State 1050-1300* (Spectrum Books, Englewood Cliffs, N.J. 1964).

INTRODUCTION

'Take note, o mighty sovereigns and incline the attention of your heart to what the good Master and Lord gave in addition to his disciple when he said, "And I will give unto thee the keys of the kingdom of heaven; whatsoever thou shalt bind on earth shall be bound also in heaven, and whatsoever thou shalt loose on earth shall be loosed in heaven". It is a very wonderful and glorious thing to bind and loose on earth and to have that sentence of binding and loosing carried out in heaven.' *The Donation of Constantine.*

I. BIOGRAPHICAL

Information is sparse about the personal life of Jean Quidort.[1] The most plausible of several conjectures about the date of his birth places it in the years 1250-54. He joined the Dominicans as a young man, whether before or after taking a master's degree in Arts in the University of Paris remains uncertain. He may well have been emerging from merely pupil status in the Parisian theological world in the later 1270's. His first major work which can be dated with any degree of confidence is his *Commentary on the Sentences* of 1284-86. Probably contemporaneously with this production, he wrote a reply to the *Correctorium fratris Thomae* of the Franciscan Walter de la Mare. This latter work, written first in 1278 and revised in 1284, was a censure of some 118 theses of Thomas Aquinas, mostly philosophical in character, alleged to be contrary to the Scrip-

---

[1] The best account of John of Paris's career, with a list of his writings and a bibliography of modern work, is F. J. Roensch, *Early Thomistic School* (Dubuque, Iowa 1964) 98-104 ; 142-48.

tures and the teachings of the Fathers. It was compulsory reading in the Franciscan schools of theology if Aquinas' *Summa theologiae* and some of his other works were being studied. John of Paris' *Correctorium 'Circa'*, a correctory of de la Mare's correctory, was one of five such works which have survived from Dominican sources in both Paris and Oxford.

These two works formed a solid basis for Quidort's academic reputation, and by 1300 he was established as one of the most prominent of the teachers and preachers of the leading theological school of Christendom. By the time of his death in September 1306, he had written on a wide variety of topics: natural philosophy, metaphysics, theology and politics. The authoritative list of his *opera omnia* contains twenty-two entries. With these works, John emerges as one of those whose common range of intellectual interests, brotherhood in religion and philosophical allegiance united to form the first school of Thomism.

John of Paris received his theological and philosophical formation in a milieu dominated by the debate about alleged radical novelties introduced by Aquinas and other neo-Aristotelians. He himself was not afraid of novelty. In the period of his *Commentary* and *Correctorium,* certain of his views concerning the Eucharist were submitted to his Master-General as fallacious. He wrote an able treatise in his own defence and emerged with nothing more serious than a postponement of his inception as master in theology. In 1304, however, the same subject brought him into more serious trouble and he was deprived of his licence to teach and preach. He was still waiting for his appeal to Pope Clement V to be heard when he died at the papal curia, then temporarily at Bordeaux.

There is little enough in this history to throw light on his interest in politics. It is clear that he had a taste for controversy. A concern for social justice and reform of the Church has been detected in his *Sermons*. But we know of no specific reason why, in the early years of the fourteenth century, he should have put his pen at the service of his king, Philip IV, then involved in a bitter clash with Pope Boniface VIII about ecclesiastical and papal powers and rights in the politics and temporal affairs of France. Nothing at all is known of his connexions with the French court beyond the fact that he was prepared to write in its support and to put his name along with all his Dominican *confrères*[2] and most of the French clergy to a petition urging Philip the Fair to arraign Boniface before a general council for his alleged misdeeds.

II. THE TREATISE'S PLACE
IN THE HISTORY OF THOUGHT

John's treatise *De potestate regia et papali* was not of course the only piece of polemical literature to be produced on the French side in the course of this controversy. It has been the unanimous opinion of historians, however, that it is much the ablest of them in its comprehensiveness of treatment and in its overall intellectual force.[3] No doubt

---

[2] Cf. P. Dondaine, "Documents pour servir à l'histoire de la province de France," *Archivum Fratrum Praedicatorum* 22 (1952) 381-439.

[3] Selecting opinion almost at random: T. S. R. Boase: "Amongst such theories the most considerable work is that of a Dominican, John of Paris..." *Boniface VIII* (London 1933) 323; C. H. McIlwain: "the longest and much the ablest of all the writings issued at this time on the King's side." *The Growth of Political Thought in the West* (New York 1934) 263; B. Tierney: "Perhaps the

there is a strong element of exaggeration in seeing John of Paris, as some have done, as the intellectual leader of the French opposition and the instigator of the seizure of Boniface VIII at Anagni.[4] But few would dispute the judgment of A. J. Carlyle that 'it serves to represent the confident and thorough-going temper in which the French king and his advisers met the claims of Boniface VIII'.[5]

It is not, however, primarily in the localized context of a particular controversy, of capital importance in itself though that undoubtedly is, that the treatise has its significance. It has a part in the whole medieval discussion of the problem of the place of the Church in politics. Indeed its relevance has not been confined only to the medieval period. As long as men have thought it worthwhile to have recourse to medieval theology and political thought for a better understanding of the relations of Church and State, John of Paris has been held in honour.

He has enjoyed the distinction of being esteemed by two politico-theological traditions of very different tendency. The six editions of his treatise which appeared between 1506 and 1683 are evidence of the keen interest shown in him by the theologians and jurists of Gallicanism.[6] John

---

greatest of all the works of political theory written at this time is the *De Potestate Regia et Papali* of the French Dominican friar John of Paris". *The Crisis of Church and State 1050-1300* (Englewood Cliffs, N.J. 1964) 195-96. Among analyses of the treatise two are of special importance: R. Scholz, *Die Publizistik zur Zeit Philipps des Schönen und Bonifaz VIII.* (Stuttgart 1903) 275-333 and J. Rivière, *Le problème de l'église et de l'état au temps de Philippe le Bel* (Louvain 1926) 148-50, 281-300. The standard work is, however, J. Leclercq, *Jean de Paris et l'ecclésiologie du XIIIᵉ siècle* (Paris 1942).

[4] Scholz, *op. cit.* 29.

[5] A. J. and R. W. Carlyle, *A History of Mediaeval Political Theory in the West* 5 (Edinburgh 1928) 437.

[6] The editions are listed in Leclercq, *op. cit.* 156 n. 3.

of Paris was preeminently one of 'our forefathers' from whom the Gallicans claimed to derive the liberties which assured the French Crown of its independence of any ecclesiastical authority in temporal affairs and the French Church of a high degree of autonomy of papal spiritual jurisdiction. They could find in his treatise too, at least some suggestions pointing towards their theory of church government which subordinated papal authority to the authority of the general council.

On the other hand, some of those who have sought a *theologia perennis* of Church-State relations, a common tradition of Christian orthodoxy, steering a course between the Charybdis of hierocracy and the Scylla of erastianism, have claimed John of Paris for their own. This tradition, rightly or wrongly, was identified particularly with Aquinas ; John of Paris, in so much else a zealous propagator and defender of Thomist doctrines, was seen as treading also in his political footsteps. This line of interpretation, first expressly formulated in 1536 by the great Jesuit theologian and controversialist Robert Bellarmine,[7], could still, over four centuries later, strike significant response in Jesuit circles.[8] It must be noticed, however, that not all modern commentators interested in Roman Catholic thought, have been so confident either about making John a moderate

---

[7] *De summo pontifice* 5.1 ed. C. Giacon, *S. Roberto Bellarmino. Scritti Politici* (Bologna 1950) 114-15. Bellarmine referred particularly to chapters 6 and 7 of the treatise as evidence that John should be aligned with those who professed the *sententia media et catholicorum theologorum communis*.

[8] Cf. J. C. Murray S.J., "Contemporary Orientations of Catholic Thought on Church and State in the Light of History," *Theological Studies* 10 (1949) 177-234.

[9] Cf. C. Journet, *L'Église du Verbe Incarné* 1 (Paris 1941) 285.

and orthodox pro-papal theorist[9] or about making his politics Thomistic.[10]

The significance of John of Paris's treatise in the history of thought is not, however, restricted to its contribution to Gallican or Jesuit or any other school of political theology. Some historians esteem it for a precisely contrary reason, for its contribution to that movement of ideas which worked towards the emancipation of politics from theology. What characterized this movement, it is argued, was its *esprit laïque,* its assault on the social and political position which the Church claimed for itself, its insistence that civil authority was autonomous, sovereign, free of any ecclesiastical coercive force, its emphasis on the natural origin of the state and that the ultimate sanction of authority was the community. Political theory was discovering the 'secular state'. With the appearance in 1324 of the *Defensor Pacis* it had found it. John of Paris, in this interpretation, was the precursor of Marsilius of Padua and the 'secularist' view of politics.[11]

III. THE CONTEXT OF THE TREATISE

The story of the clash between Boniface VIII and Philip the Fair is a familiar enough one: this was one of

[10] Cf. M. F. Griesbach, "John of Paris as a Representative of Thomistic Political Philosophy" in *An E. Gilson Tribute* ed. C. J. O'Neill (Milwaukee 1959) 33-50.

[11] The interpretation is stated in its baldest terms by J. Bowle, *Western Political Thought* (London 1947) 203. More nuanced analyses of the John of Paris — Marsilius of Padua liaison may be found in G. de Lagarde, *La naissance de l'esprit laïque au déclin du moyen-âge* 1 (Paris 1948) 254-59; A. Gewirth, *Marsilius of Padua The Defender of Peace* 2 (New York 1956) xlvi-lii; W. Ullmann, *Principles of Government and Politics in the Middle Ages* (London 1961) 231-79.

the classic Church-State duels of the middle ages. But some recapitulation of its evolution, its main documents and statements of principle is essential background to our treatise. There is much more to be learned about it from the events of Franco-papal relations than from the *curriculum vitae* of John of Paris.

It is a story told, conventionally, in two parts.[12] The first, beginning with the promulgation by Boniface VIII of *Clericis laicos* on 24 February 1296 and ending with his *Etsi de statu* of 31 July 1297, was but a skirmish preliminary to the main battle. This was joined after the arrest of Bernard Saisset, bishop of Pamiers, by royal officers in October 1301, with the issuing early in the following December of *Salvator mundi* and *Ausculta Fili* and culminated with the seizure of Boniface VIII by Guillaume de Nogaret at Anagni on 7 September 1303, one day in advance of that fixed for the formal promulgation of *Super Petri solio* solemnly excommunicating Philip. Boniface died some six weeks later (20 October 1303). The juridical axiom *mors omnia solvit* was not to apply in his case. Philip IV continued down to 1311 to threaten to press charges of heresy, simony, usurpation of the papacy and other matters against Boniface, trial to take place in a general council.

It was to be the second act of the drama which pro-

---

[12] An excellent introduction is C. T. Wood ed. *Philip the Fair and Boniface VIII* (New York 1967). The standard book is G. Digard, *Philippe le Bel et le Saint Siège de 1285 à 1304*, 2 vols. (Paris 1936), containing extensive translations from the sources. V. Martin, *Les origines du Gallicanisme* 1 (Paris 1939) is useful. Except where otherwise stated the sources cited here may be consulted in P. Dupuy, *Histoire du différend d'entre le pape Boniface VIII et Philippe le Bel...* (Paris 1655 : Tucson, Ariz. 1963).

duced the most radical confrontation of two different political theories in a clash about sovereignty. The events of 1296-7 formed a prologue to this clash. Dispute in those years centred round the relatively narrow issue of the right of a king to tax the property of his clergy. A well-established papal principle, in its final formulation dating from Innocent III's Fourth Lateran Council of 1215, ruled that a secular power might not tax church *temporalia* without first obtaining permission from the pope. This was binding on pain of excommunication for those who demanded and those who paid when licence had not been granted. It had been the ordinary practice of the kings of France to give heed to this principle. Philip IV himself had observed it on at least one important occasion, when in 1288 he had been granted a tenth for a period of three years. Under the severe pressure of the demands of his war with Edward I, however, Philip had dispensed with the formality and had thereby given cause for clerical protest from France to Rome. *Clericis laicos* was a reminder to lay rulers of the traditional principle. It seems clear that Boniface was not intent on making trouble with France and was surprised by the vigour of the French reaction. Impelled by the hostility of the French government and by pressure from the French clergy for a compromise, Boniface back-pedalled in a series of bulls in which he tried to maintain the traditional principle whilst making a series of exceptions from it designed to meet the demands of the French king and clergy. Finally, in *Etsi de statu,* Boniface allowed levies from the clergy in defence of the kingdom (of whose need the king was to be the judge) without papal authorization. It also permitted the clergy to make voluntary gifts without such authorization. *Clericis laicos* had been circumvented and, as had generally been the case in Franco-papal relations, the French king had had his way. In all this there was no major crisis in France comparable to the position in England where *Clericis laicos* had led Edward I, in an exactly parallel financial predicament to Philip IV's, to the extreme step of outlawing his clergy.[13]

This first dispute did not spark off any great spate of theorizing about the relations of the powers as the second conflict was to do. But in the period of its course, both parties took occasion to state at least their minimum claims. Boniface VIII's *Ineffabilis amor* (20 September 1296) had threatened that a violator of ecclesiastical liberty — one who laid hands on churchmen or their property — would be excommunicated. It also asserted (echo of Innocent III's *Novit*) that should some other king accuse Philip of sin, its judgment would pertain to the apostolic see.[14] Philip, for his part, left no room for doubt where he stood. In matters pertaining to his soul and the *spiritualitas*, he was prepared humbly and devoutly to obey the warnings and precepts of the apostolic see, as his forefathers had done. But the temporal *regimen* of his kingdom belonged to him alone and as far as that was concerned he recognized no superior whatsoever.[15] The second conflict was to bring these principles, in all their logical development, into head-on collision.

The issue at stake was sovereignty. There is no need to have scruples about whether the use of this word, so

---

[13] Cf. F. M. Powicke, *The Thirteenth Century* (Oxford 1962), 615.

[14] *Régistres de Boniface VIII* ed. G. Digard *et al.* (Bibl. des écoles françaises d'Athènes et de Rome 1884-1931) no. 1653.

[15] Cf. J. Gaudemet in *Histoire des institutions françaises au moyen-âge*, t. 3 Institutions ecclésiastiques (Paris 1962) 324.

much discussed in modern times, in a medieval context
is anachronistic. The word already had its place in the
French political vocabulary.[16] It appeared first, to all
seeming, in the early twelfth century, where *suvrainetet*
deriving from medieval Latin *superanus* meant the summit
of any elevated place, as for instance of mountains. In
addition to this physical connotation, it was used in the
moral sense of elevated or superior. It was thus easily
extended to the one who in society and in law was elevated
over the community, superior to all its members. Hence
the king was 'sovereign lord' and antonomastically 'sovereign'. In the treatises of thirteenth-century French lawyers,
the king was 'souverain es choses temporeix' who has no
'souverain es choses temporeix' (*Etablissements de S.
Louis*)[17] to whom judicial appeals might be made 'par
reson de la sovraineté' (Beaumanoir). Rendered into the
Latin of the schools 'sovereignty' in the sense of supreme
temporal authority became 'ius summae superioritatis in
regno suo'.[18] The second conflict between Philip the Fair
and Boniface VIII was about this *summa superioritas,* royal
sovereignty.

It began with the arrest in October 1301 of Bernard
Saisset who had become the first bishop of Pamiers in
1295. Bernard was loud-mouthed, unsympathetic to the
king and careless alike of who knew it and of what

---

[16] Cf. P. Robert, *Dictionnaire alphabétique et analogique de la Langue française*;
F. Godefroy, *Dict. de l'ancienne langue franç.* ; O. Bloch and W. von Wartburg,
Dict. étymologique de la langue franç.; E. Littré, *Dict. de la langue franç.*

[17] 2.14 (ed. P. Viollet, Paris 1881-1886, t. 2, p. 369).

[18] This term occurred in the anonymous treatise *Rex Pacificus* ed. Dupuy,
Histoire, 675.

enemies he made. With war in Gascony, the area was politically extremely sensitive and the Bishop was denounced to the king as a traitor. After investigation, Bernard was arrested and his property sequestrated. When he was charged before Pierre Flotte, the royal chancellor, accusations of simony, heresy and blasphemy had been added to the original charge of treason. Saisset was committed to the custody of his metropolitan, the archbishop of Narbonne. At this stage, Philip prepared to take up the matter with Boniface VIII on the basis of negociating an agreed procedure for the further conduct of a case for which there were no particular French precedents.

The explosion of papal wrath that followed was not merely the product of a choleric temperament. To Boniface it came as the last intolerable incident in a succession of violations of the jurisdictional and fiscal liberties of the Church in France. The shelter given in France to the Cardinals James and Peter Colonna, excommunicated and expelled from the Sacred College, now violently attacking the validity of Boniface's election, his character and the conduct of his government, was particularly provocative. The whole of the proceedings against Bernard Saisset violated, to Boniface's mind, the traditional Franco-papal understanding of the privileged position of a bishop in relation to secular jurisdiction. It was a sufficiently important principle on which to decide that the time had come to take a stand against Philip IV.

The Pope's first step was to suspend all the privileges granted by the apostolic see to France. He had in mind especially those alleviations of the strict principle of clerical fiscal immunity as laid down in *Clericis laicos*. He ordered the archbishop of Narbonne to have Saisset released forthwith. He then proceeded to initiate action against the person and policies of Philip IV. The bull *Ausculta fili* (5 December 1301)[19] is perhaps the most fundamental and revealing of all Boniface's fulminations against the king of France. It contains at once the basic theologico-political axioms on which rested the ultimate justification for Boniface's claim to authority over Philip as well as all the technical legal particularities of the specific issues of the quarrel. It is a much better revelation of Boniface's mind than the better known *Clericis laicos* and *Unam sanctam*.

Philip should read *Ausculta fili,* Boniface bade him, as the expression of the Pope's paternal, and the Church's maternal, love for him. Boniface called his letter a *sermo* and so in part it was: a stern admonition to remember his Christian inheritance, his duty to reform to avoid God's fearful punishments and an exhortation to undertake that standard penance for errant kings, the neglected cause of the Holy Land. But *Ausculta fili* was not merely the rebuke of a stern father. Much more significantly, it was the accusation of a judge. The King was being accused by the vicar of Christ who commanded that ark of Noah, the universal Church outside of which there was no salvation, in virtue of the *primatus* granted with the keys of Peter which made him judge of the living and the dead. God had set his vicar over kings and kingdoms. The scriptural allusion here (Jeremias 1.10) carried a double implication. It referred to the pastoral ministry of souls committed to the shepherd of the Lord's flock. But it also referred to the coercive jurisdiction granted to the head of the Church

---

[19] *Reg.* no. 4424.

to punish, by excommunication and deposition, those who disobeyed him. When Boniface adjured Philip, 'not to let anyone persuade him that he had no superior, that he was not subject to the head of the ecclesiastical hierarchy' he was not referring to himself merely as spiritual father and pastoral shepherd. He was emphasising his superiority as one with power to judge, sentence and coerce a ruler. These generalities about the nature and origin of papal jurisdiction were to be reiterated in more detail in *Unam sanctam*.

There followed a detailed list of Philip's alleged crimes: abuse of the privilege of collating to benefices, thereby derogating papal right, for it was only by papal consent that the King had power to collate; injury and molestation of churchmen in their persons and property through usurpation of ecclesiastical jurisdiction; misuse of episcopal property during vacancies; injustice to the clergy through the prohibition of the taking of money out of the kingdom; debasing the coinage.

In the third part of *Ausculta fili* Boniface revealed what practical steps he intended taking against Philip IV. 'Since you have stopped your ears to the healing admonitions, like the deaf asp of which the Psalmist has spoken (Ps. 57.5),' he continued, 'I must take further steps to save your soul and preserve the common welfare of your kingdom.' Hence there were to be summoned to Rome all the prelates of France, heads of religious orders, representatives of cathedral chapters, masters of theology and law to give advice as to what should be done to rectify wrongs and reform the King. Furthermore, and this is the really significant part, these churchmen would be required to treat of the 'peace and well-being, the good and just government of the kingdom itself'. Clearly the supreme judge was assembling his court. Judgment was to be on nothing less than the conduct of the king's government. There can be no shadow of doubt as to what Boniface considered was the ultimate sanctions of his judgments in such a matter. For later, he was to 'recall' to the French ambassadors in public consistory that 'our predecessors deposed three kings of France ... if the king were to commit the same crimes as they committed or greater ones, we would depose him as if he were but a squire (*sicut garcionem*)'. Who was then 'souverain es choses temporeix' in France, if this judge really had the competence he claimed?

Philip the Fair and his advisers were short neither of ideas nor of support in their counters to this papal threat to French independence. A much quoted anecdote about Pierre Flotte has the King's chancellor telling Boniface that while his power was merely *verbalis* that of his master's was *realis*.[20] If by this he meant that the King could exercise a degree of physical force denied to the Pope, he was of course quite right. And it was violence which won the day when the seizure of Boniface at Anagni undoubtedly hastened his death and the arrival on the papal throne of successors pliant towards the French king to the point of servility. But for all his final reliance on force, the King did go to great lengths to mount a defence of his position in the realm of ideas.

His most immediate need was to prevent the French hierarchy from giving whole-hearted support to Boniface. Thus his first objective was to stifle the effectiveness of

[20] Cf. Rivière, *op. cit.* 121 n. 2.

the council of French bishops. Through his chancellor Pierre
Flotte he employed a simple tactic to discredit the November Rome council project. He represented it to a meeting
of the Estates (April 1302) as the practical implementation
of the Pope's alleged view that France was subject to him
temporaliter, a kingdom held by its kings, not as everyone
had hitherto always assumed, from God, but from the
papacy. This was a prelude to a wholesale attack on
Boniface as an enemy of France who had misused his
power over the French Church. Philip asked for the cooperation of his people, represented in the Estates, to
reject the excessive political claims of Boniface VIII and
sought to rally them to his support in the defense of the
liberties and honour of France.

It is more than likely that the ground had already been
prepared for the reception of this propaganda by the cir-
culation of a document purporting to be of papal origin,
which reads like an over-forced summary of *Ausculta fili.*
It ran as follows:

> Fear God (*Deum time*) and keep his commandments.
> We want you to know that you are subject to us in
> spiritual and temporal matters. The collation of benefices
> and prebends is none of your business. And if you have
> custody of temporalities during vacancies, you should
> reserve the income for those who succeed to the offices
> in question. Should you have collated, we declare the
> act null; if it has taken place, revoke it. Those who
> believe otherwise, we hold to be heretics.

To this, the King was alleged to have replied:

> Let your high folly know (*Sciat tua maxima fatuitas*)
> that we are not subject to anyone in temporal affairs, that
> collation of vacant churches and prebends belongs to us

> of royal right, that their revenues are for us, that collations
> made in the past or to be made in the future are valid
> and we shall strenuously protect those who hold them.
> Those who believe otherwise, we hold to be fools and
> madmen.

These assertions and counter-assertions were to focus a
good deal of the arguments of the politico-theological treatises written in University circles and of the speeches of
royal counsellors.

On their own account to the Pope, the French clergy
tried to avoid committing themselves to any positive stand
in support of the King, but were not able to withstand his
pressure. They had rejected, they claimed, the assertion that
the Pope had deliberately set himself to do harm to the
kingdom, and they had humbly asked the King for permission to go to the Rome council. This he had refused. The
clergy asked the Pope to preserve the traditional harmony
of Church and Crown in France by withdrawing his sum-
mons to the council.

The baronage and third estate showed no comparable
sense of embarrassment at being caught between two loyalties. They rallied enthusiastically to Philip. They spoke up
strongly against Boniface's alleged pretension that he
might put a principle of temporal sovereignty over France
into the practice of summoning a council to judge the
conduct of its king. They reiterated with gusto the charges
of oppression of the French Church. They lectured the
Pope on what was, and what was not, pleasing to God.

Through letters from the cardinals to both estates of the
laity and from the Pope to the prelates, the curia replied to
all these statements. Any claim to papal sovereignty of
France *temporaliter* was denied, and so too was any sugges-

tion that kings of France held their kingdom, not from God, but from the papacy. Charges of misuse by the curia of provisions in France were convincingly refuted. The spirit and teaching of *Ausculta fili* was defended and re-stated. The right of the papacy to summon the council was also defended and based firmly on the traditional principle which Innocent III had put into classical terminology when in controversy with another king of France about a century earlier: 'No one in his right mind can deny that the pope, head of the Church, supreme hierarch, can judge any man for reason of sin (*ratione peccati*)'.

The principle that Philip the Fair was indictable before the Pope *ratione peccati* runs like a red thread through the whole dispute. It was to be taken up again in June of 1302 when *Ausculta fili* was again defended and *Deum time* disowned, this time in consistory in the presence of French ambassadors. 'It is plain', said the official spokesman, Cardinal Matthew Aquasparta, 'that no one can call into doubt the principle that the pope can judge in every temporal matter *ratione peccati*.' It was also plain that the Cardinal's understanding of this jurisdiction in fact came perilously close to what *Deum time* had said was Boniface's principle of the temporal subjection of the French kingdom and the derivation of its jurisdiction from the papacy. Matthew of Aquasparta explained himself in these terms:

> In the Church which is the barque of Christ and of Peter, there is said to be one ruler and one head whose command everyone is bound to obey and he who has the plenitude of power is said to be lord of all things temporal and spiritual (cf. Ps. 23.1) as will later appear more clearly ... Further, it is plain that no one can call into doubt the

principle that the pope can judge in every temporal matter *ratione peccati*. It is written that God created two great lights, a greater to illumine the day and a lesser to illumine the night. Thus there are two jurisdictions, spiritual and temporal, the pope has the spiritual jurisdiction, given by Christ to Peter and to the popes, his successors; the temporal jurisdiction is held by the emperor and other kings. Yet the pope has cognizance and judgment of every temporal matter *ratione peccati*. Hence my argument is: temporal jurisdiction may be viewed either so far as it pertains to anyone in act and usage or so far as it pertains by right. Thus, temporal jurisdiction belongs of right to the pope, who is vicar of Christ and of Peter; anyone who asserts the contrary impugns that article of the creed, 'He shall judge the living and the dead' and also 'the communion of the saints'. But as far as usage of temporal jurisdiction is concerned, its executive action that is to say, this does not belong to the pope since Peter was instructed, 'Put up thy sword into its sheath'. In this way, it may be seen that the French king has no ground for complaint.

Pope Boniface VIII also spoke on the same occasion. His address was characterized by an especially vigorous denunciation of Pierre Flotte, 'a man of the devil', who, it was claimed, had misrepresented the pope's letter to the King, or had caused it to be falsified, to spread the lie that the pope was ordering the King to acknowledge that he held his kingdom from the pope. Boniface protested vehemently that as a veteran of forty years experience of the canon law it was inconceivable for him to commit himself to such a fatuous error: 'We know very well that God has established two powers. We affirm that we have no desire whatsoever to usurp the royal jurisdiction, as our brother the cardinal bishop of Porto (Matthew of Aquasparta) has said. But the king cannot deny, any more than any Christian can deny, that he is subject to us *ratione peccati*.' He went on to affirm that the right to collate to benefices was an exclusively ecclesiastical matter, though he professed himself willing to continue to accommodate the king in this regard, as indeed, he claimed, he had done in the past. He protested his love for France and for the King personally, an attachment of long standing which had been, he claimed, of great service to Philip in the past. His speech ended on a note of menace: 'Our predecessors deposed three kings of France. The French can read of it in their chronicles, just as we can in ours and one case is to be found in the *Decretum* ... if the king were to commit the same crimes as they committed or greater ones, we would depose him as if he were but a squire ...'. Finally, he insisted that the French prelates should come to the council he had summoned for November 'because we have heard that kingdom to be desolate among all the kingdoms of the world. And because there is no health in it from the soles of the feet to the crown of the head ... every bishop must come and will be deposed if he absents himself without cause.'

Exact dating of the *On royal and papal power* is not possible.[21] But we can be reasonably confident that John of Paris was abreast of the events so far narrated, at least in their main outlines. For his treatise shows unmistakeable traces of *Ausculta fili* and *Deum time*, as well as clear evidence that he knew of the papal and royal

---

[21] Dom Leclercq has discussed the dating problem in detail, *op. cit.* 10-14 to conclude: "La date approximative de notre traité reste la fin de 1302 ou les premiers mois de 1303; il paraît impossible de préciser davantage."

attitudes to the Rome council. It would not be safe to
deduce, however, that he had knowledge of the council
itself or of its aftermath. Considerable significance must be
attached to the absence of any reference to *Unam sanctam*.
Promulgated on 18 November 1302, sole important product of the Rome council, it was the culmination of the
papal ideology and provoked considerable hostility in
France. It is difficult to envisage John of Paris knowing
of this most controversial document and failing to refer to
it, at least indirectly. Nor is there any unambiguous reference to any event or document later than *Unam sanctam*.
It seems very likely therefore, that the treatise had been
finished before the autumn of 1302, almost a year, that is
to say, before the seizure of Boniface VIII and his death in
October 1303.

Nevertheless, some consideration of the development of
the controversy in its last months is necessary background
for the full understanding of the treatise. Two lines of
thought and action demand attention. It will be seen later
that much of the treatise is concerned to combat the arguments of the protagonists of papal authority. Some analysis
of *Unam sanctam* is called for, at least for purposes of
comparison with John's statement of the papal case, to
estimate how far it is an accurate and up-to-date presentation of it. For *Unam sanctam* sought to put that case in
its most official form. The second development calling for
notice comes from the other side of the dispute. In 1303,
the French began to call for the arrest of Boniface VIII
and for his trial before a general council. His capture at
Anagni may be seen as judicial arrest before this trial.
Even after the Pope's death, the French government continued for many years to threaten to implement this threat

of trial. French politicians were prepared to disregard the orthodox principle of papal immunity from human judgment. French theologians had already explored the arguments justifying conciliar and lay action against a pope held to be unsuitable for his office. John of Paris was perhaps the most venturesome of such explorers.

When the canonists came to give *Unam sanctam* its place in the *Corpus Iuris Canonici,* they summarized it with the rubric: 'All Christ's faithful, of necessity of salvation, are subject to the Roman pontiff who has both swords, judges all, but himself is judged by no one'. This was to pinpoint very accurately the four major emphases of the bull.

The first principle mentioned was the most important as far as the general tenor of the bull was concerned. *Unam sanctam* was about obedience: it was written to declare as an article of faith that obedience to the pope was a necessity of salvation. The main proof offered was the papal jurisdictional power, the commission of the keys to St. Peter:

> This authority although granted to man and exercised by man, is not human but divine, being given to Peter by the voice of God and confirmed to him and to his successors in him, the rock whom the Lord acknowledged when he said to Peter, 'Whatsoever thou shalt bind etc.' Whoever, therefore, resists this power ordained of God resists the ordinance of God.

There was nothing new about the doctrine. A standard gloss on Matthew 16.19, of Origen, collected by Aquinas in his *Catena aurea,* spoke of Peter's judgments being 'as if God is judging through Peter's power' (*quasi Deo iudicante per eam*). Canonistic variations of the theme were common-place. That it was necessary to remain obedient to save one's soul was likewise well-known. Gregory VII, for example, in one of the most celebrated of his political letters had stated it:

> Who, I ask, can consider himself exempt from this universal power granted to Peter of binding and loosing unless perchance that unfortunate who, unwilling to bear the yoke of the Lord, subjects himself to the burden of the devil and refuses to be numbered with the sheep of Christ?[22]

Boniface VIII chose different words. His formula came ultimately from the Pseudo-Cyril, *Liber Thesaurorum* (now lost), possibly by way of Aquinas' *Contra Graecos* or just conceivably by way of James of Viterbo's *De regimine christiano*.[23]

Much of *Unam sanctam,* particularly its long opening paragraph, was concerned with general principles of ecclesiology, with especial reference to the unity of the Church. When it eventually became specifically political, the argument was organized round the metaphor of the two swords, deriving from Luke 22.38. Boniface VIII was here consciously using the language of St. Bernard of Clairvaux, language which had become the established terminology of the schools. The principle the Pope was expounding had been put very succinctly, for example, by Aquinas: 'The Church has also the temporal sword at its command: because at its command, it must be drawn, as Bernard said'.[24]

---

[22] *Registrum Gregorii VII* ed. E. Caspar (MGH) VIII. 21, p. 548.

[23] Cf. my *The Theory of Papal Monarchy in the Thirteenth Century* (New York-London 1965) 91 n. 5.

[24] *Commentary on the Sentences* 4. d. 37 exp. text.

Boniface and his theological advisers (Aegidius Romanus was the foremost of them) might have chosen many authorities to demonstrate the classical papal claim to judicial omnicompetence with papal immunity from human judgment. It is characteristic of *Unam sanctam* that despite Boniface's expertise as a canonist, it avoided canonical authorities, choosing wherever possible a scriptural text, even when its literal context was not necessarily a papal one. In this instance it was a text of St. Paul (1 Cor. 2.15) which was pressed into service: 'The spiritual man judgeth all things and he himself is judged of no one'. This usage of the text was not traditional. But it was well known in early decretist circles. Huguccio, for example, had used it in this sense and it is, therefore, not surprising to find his pupil, Innocent III adopting it too.[25]

Going on to reinforce the point that judgment of all meant also that the spiritual power might judge the temporal power, the bull had recourse to the twelfth century theologian Hugh of St. Victor: 'The truth bearing witness, it is for the spiritual power to establish (*instituere*) the temporal power and to judge it if it do wrong'. This statement had gained some popularity in the thirteenth century, being reproduced in the *Summa theologiae* of Alexander of Hales and thence in the *Apparatus* of the great canonist, Hostiensis. Allegedly establishing this proposition was Jeremias 1.10, 'I have this day set thee over the nations and over kingdoms'. It had been Innocent III

---

[25] Huguccio on *Decretum* 2 q. 7 c. 41 *s.v. nostro iuditio* (unpublished); Innocent III, *Sermo III in consecratione pontificis maximi* PL 217.658. It was in use, too, among the papalists of Boniface VIII's time, cf. James Viterbo, *De regimine christiano* ed. H. X. Arquillière (Paris 1926) 207.

who had claimed this text as a prefiguration of the Petrine commission of the keys. Others went further. Hostiensis interpreted it as a justification of a papal deposing power.[26]

All in all, *Unam sanctam* was a very fair reflexion of the post-Gregorian phase of papal ideology. It was not likely, however, to soothe any French susceptibilities.

By the spring of 1303, the French attitude to the Pope had hardened considerably. At a *parlement* held in the Louvre in March, Guillaume de Nogaret made a violent attack on Boniface, accusing him *inter alia* of usurpation of the apostolic see, heresy and simony. He demanded that the Pope should be suspended from office until a general council had been summoned to condemn 'this infamous criminal' and to provide the Church with a legitimate pastor. This was not idle talk. Nogaret left secretly for Italy to seize Boniface. In June at a new *parlement,* his replacement, Guillaume de Plaisian initiated the first formal judicial step in the trial of Boniface. The generalized accusations made by Nogaret in March were particularized into twenty-nine specific accusations. Plaisian announced that he would be the prosecutor at a trial, for choice by general council, but envisaging the possibility of some other court.

There were twenty-one bishops present and numerous senior religious. They declared that having heard what Plaisian had had to say they thought the convocation of a general council necessary either for Boniface to demonstrate his innocence or to have judgment passed on him. They protested their willingness to cooperate in the summoning of a general council and announced their intention of

---

[26] Cf. *Theory of Papal Monarchy* 39-41; 57-58; 127.

appealing to a future general council and to a future legitimate pope should Boniface excommunicate or suspend them. In the months that followed, royal officials toured the kingdom collecting similar pledges of cooperation from those who mattered politically and ecclesiastically. John of Paris, along with the other French Dominicans, was among the signatories. But when the process against Boniface did actually begin (though it was not to be brought to a conclusion) on 16 March 1310, John of Paris was already dead.[27]

IV. STRUCTURE, SOURCES, METHODOLOGY

John of Paris was making a contribution to a debate about the political implications of sacerdotal and papal power and there was a conventional method of going about such analyses. University men had a standard technique for handling controversial topics. They used the method of dialectic which supplied a basic framework for the argument to proceed. In essence, there were four parts: arguments were arranged for and against the proposition or *quaestio,* a conclusion was reached, and finally reply was made to the arguments which had been rejected. The format could be followed in different degrees of length and elaboration according to the interest and skill of the writer. Two such *quaestiones* have survived from this period. The *Quaestio in utramque partem* offers a classical example of this method adapted to the discussion

---

[27] For the trial, cf. G. Lizerand, *Clément V et Philippe le Bel* (Paris 1910); G. Mollat, *Les papes d'Avignon* (10th edn. Paris 1964) 402-406.

of the Franco-papal controversy.[28] The two sides of the *quaestio* were represented, respectively, by *Deum time* and by its reply *Sciat tua maxima fatuitas*. The arguments for each case were put forward, a position established which powerfully upheld the sovereignty of the king of Frence, arguments in favour of a papal power *in temporalibus* were destroyed whilst, however, leaving the spiritual authority of the papacy intact, and even conceding it a certain degree of political jurisdiction in certain circumstances. *Rex pacificus* was constructed on the same model and used very similar materials, though its conclusions were not identical.[29] The structure, sources and methodology of the *On royal and papal power* is much of a type with these two works, though it is more elaborate, more comprehensive and more radical than either.

In the Proemium of his treatise, John of Paris specified as his main objective the discovery of the truth about sacerdotal power *in temporalibus*. The first ten chapters, treating of the general principles of ecclesiastical and civil power, were devoted to establishing that no lordship or jurisdiction had been given to prelates in virtue of their office as vicars of Christ and successors of the Apostles. Chapter 11 rehearsed the arguments which the author had 'read and heard' advanced in favour of the contrary position. When the author of the *Quaestio in utramque partem* had compiled a comparable list he discovered twenty such arguments, while the author of *Rex pacificus* found seven-

---

[28] Cf. my "The Quaestio in utramque partem reconsidered," *Studia Gratiana* 13 (1967) 411-54.

[29] For the most recent analysis, W. Ullmann, "A Medieval Document on Papal Theories of Government," *E.H.R.* (1946) 180-201.

teen. John of Paris' list has forty-two entries to form a thoroughly representative statement, including some that were used in *Unam sanctam*. Chapters 12 and 13 propound the author's conclusion from the confrontation of the two positions. They reiterate the general principles of the opening ten chapters, deepening them particularly as regards sacerdotal power *in se*. These chapters constitute the most personal part of his thinking about the problem and are the heart of the treatise. Chapters 14 to 20 reply, often in great detail, to each of the forty-two arguments advanced in Chapter 11 in favour of papal jurisdiction in temporal affairs. This is sane, balanced, convincing criticism.

It would have been quite logical for John of Paris to have stopped at this point, the examination of his problem completed. But he chose to add five more chapters, appendices, so to say, concerned with particular points about papal power which he thought better treated outside the main course of his argument. Chapter 21 examined what power had been granted to the pope by the donation of Constantine, especially in relation to the king of France. Chapter 22 was in effect an anticipation of criticism, meeting in advance the objection that the papacy as an institution was above and beyond critical examination of the principles and practice of its jurisdiction. The final three chapters formed a *quaestiunculum* about whether a pope might abdicate, a problem which had been discussed in the Parisian schools since 1292 and was now an issue of polemic against Boniface VIII. It was especially in these last chapters that John of Paris expounded his views about the circumstances in which a pope might be deposed.

'Il reste', Dom Jean Leclercq has written of John of Paris, 'qu'il appartenait à une époque où il était encore

impossible de faire de la théologie sans connaître le droit.'
Dom Leclercq was answering his own question: 'Un Jean
de Paris est-il en premier lieu un canoniste ou un théologien?'[30] His question and observation signify a major
shift in the interpretation of the treatise, for the classical
historians of this period of medieval political literature did
not attach much importance to John of Paris as canonist.
Scholz in his long analysis of the work made only passing
reference to canon law. Carlyle scarcely mentioned it.
Rivière, content to see John of Paris as simply 'théologien
et philosophe, nourri d'Aristote aussi bien que de S. Thomas' ignored it altogether.

If a full table of authors cited in the treatise were to be
compiled, it would show that by far and away the most
important single source cited was the Bible. John of Paris
was of course by training a theologian, and as part of that
training had been a teacher as well as a student of Scripture.
It was natural for him to give his political problem a
theological format and this he did by laying his chief stress
on the nature of the priesthood. The very nature of his
question demanded that the Bible should be his chief
primary source. John cited directly some 150 different
texts (sometimes of course more than once), fifty-one from
the Old Testament, ninety-nine from the New.[31] In
addition to these direct citations, there were frequent indirect scriptural allusions. Like every schoolman, John read
his Bible along with the standard commentaries, of which
the most important were the *glossa ordinaria* and the *glossa*

---

[30] "Deux questions de Berthaud de Saint-Denys sur l'exemption fiscale du
clergé," *Études d'histoire du droit canonique dédiées à G. Le Bras* 1 (Paris 1965) 607.
[31] They have been listed by Bleienstein, *op. cit.* 359-60.

interlinearis. In addition, he used the *Historia Scholastica* of Petrus Comestor, a type of Bible history, the *Catena aurea* of Aquinas on the Gospels and his Commentary on St. Paul's Epistles. These books were great collections of authoritative interpretations from many hands from many periods of exegetical history. Almost all the Patristic names which occur in the treatise are in connexion with biblical exegesis and John's knowledge of their work comes from one or other of the standard books mentioned. To complete the shelf of reference books of scriptural and theological learning, John of Paris had that major compendium on which he had written a commentary, the *Sentences* of Peter Lombard. Mention must be made too of another reference book much used by John, the *Speculum Historiale* of his Dominican predecessor, Vincent of Beauvais, a major source for both ecclesiastical and secular history.

Numerically the second largest batch of citations in the treatise came from Canon Law: fifty texts of Gratian's *Decretum* and seventeen of the Gregorian decretals, many cited more than once. It is clear that the treatise rested on the double foundations of the Bible read in the light of the standard books of the exegetes and the *Corpus Iuris Canonici* read along with the text books of the canonist schools, in particular the *glossae ordinariae*. The one provided the underlying principles of perennial validity, the other the evidence of their implementation in the life of the Church through the ages. The *Decretum* stood as a great repository of the Church's governmental experience beside which contemporary institutions, practices and principles could be put to the test. The *Decretales* recorded that experience in the most recent phase of the Church's history. Political theory, for the theological faculty at

Paris in the time of John of Paris, was essentially an amalgam of theology and canon law, representing respectively the theory and practice of authority.

There is, however, rather more to the analysis of a writer's intellectual workshop than merely counting the number of citations of this or that authority, valuable enough though that information may be in itself. For sometimes the importance of an individual writer or of an intellectual tradition on the author under review is not reflected in any very considerable number of direct acknowledged citations. And at other times, medieval authors being the plagiarists they were, writers whose influence was very great were being transcribed often word for word, without acknowledgment by name at all.

When the *On royal and papal power* is examined with these considerations in mind, two conclusions emerge. In the first place, the legacy of the Ancient World is of more significance than the relatively limited number of citations of Aristotle and Roman law might suggest. Secondly, Dom Leclercq has estimated that something like a third of the treatise is borrowed, with scarcely any alteration, from theologians who wrote either just before him or were his contemporaries. Nothing of this borrowing is acknowledged. No contemporary or near-contemporary name is mentioned, with the exception of Henry of Cremona, cited as an adversary.

The heritage of the pagan past could constitute, after the Bible and canon law, the third great bloc of source material available to the early fourteenth century political writer. For the most part, this heritage consisted of Roman law as christianized first in Justinian's codification and second in some two centuries of scholarship in the law schools of the

Latin West. By John of Paris' day, the thought of Rome, transmitted through its most characteristic monument, was an integral part of Western civilization and a major ingredient of any discussion of law, authority and the common weal, even when the writer was not a technical jurist. By contrast, Aristotelian philosophy was a much more recent arrival on the intellectual scene and its influence on medieval political writing was as yet only beginning. The Christian Aristotelianism of Aquinas was used in the Bonifacian controversy both to support the papal position, by James of Viterbo in particular,[32] and to help to criticize it, by John of Paris especially.[33] For John there was a harmony between elements he found in both Roman law and Greek philosophy. They reinforced the 'natural' part of his politics to be integrated with the 'super-natural' part supplied by the Bible and the canons. The number of literal citations of Roman law, of Cicero, of Aristotle does not do justice to the significance of the Roman and Greek contribution to the naturalistic sector of the treatise.

That John of Paris was a member of the oldest school of Thomists has already been noticed. The name of Aquinas does not, however, figure in the *On royal and papal power*. Nevertheless it has not been difficult to establish textual correspondences between it and different works of the Angelic Doctor. The extent of the borrowing, particularly in connexion with his discussion of the nature and origin

---

[32] Arquillière, *op. cit.* 72-77.
[33] W. Ullmann, *A History of Political Thought. The Middle Ages* (1965). Cf. G. Leff, "The Apostolic Ideal in Later Medieval Ecclesiology," *Journal of Theological Studies* 18 (1967) 58-82 for a powerful argument that "the role of Aristotle in later medieval political thinking has... been not only exaggerated but misconceived."

of the priesthood and of political society, is not in doubt. There is, however, a certain difference of opinion among modern commentators as to how Thomistic the treatise really is. One appreciation would see John of Paris as a 'faithful disciple' of Aquinas.[34] Another has concluded that though there is undoubtedly usage of matter supplied by Aquinas this is so edited and selected as to produce conclusions strikingly different from those of Aquinas. It would be conceded that there are some points of agreement. But it is denied that 'in its essential nature or its spirit' it constitutes a genuine expression of Aquinas's doctrine.[35] Perhaps no final settlement of this difference of opinion is possible. For in the absence of a systematic treatise by Aquinas about the relations of the two powers, there are too many ambiguities in his doctrine and too many unanswerable questions about what he did or did not hold. But it is certainly difficult to envisage Aquinas taking so critical, even defiant, a stand against currently accepted papal positions as did John of Paris.[36]

The mark of two other theologians who had adorned the University of Paris is to be discerned in the treatise. The *Quodlibeta* of Godfrey of Fontaines gave John of Paris significant sections of his chapters 6 and 7 dealing with papal lordship of lay property and contributed, too, to his discussion of papal abdication. Even more important in this latter context was the *De renuntiatione papae* of

---

[34] Leclercq, *op. cit.* 85, 97, 149.

[35] M. F. Griesbach, *art. cit.* 47.

[36] Nevertheless one would have much sympathy for the view that "it is likely that the Dominican John of Paris was closer than the Augustinian Giles of Rome to St. Thomas's political temper" : T. Gilby, *St. Thomas Aquinas Summa Theologiae*, vol. 28 *Law and Political Theory* (London 1966) xxiv.

Aegidius Romanus. For considerable parts of chapters 23 to 25, John of Paris was merely summarizing this book. But the insertion of his own personal conclusions about papal deposition here, so very different in temper from Aegidius Romanus,' is a clear-cut single illustration of the general judgment that John of Paris was no mindless transmitter of other people's work. Dom Leclercq's over-all assessment is assuredly correct: 'S'il emprunte à ses sources beaucoup d'idées, il les assimile à sa pensée au point de se les rendre vraiment personnelles: son originalité en est à peine diminuée, et son mérite reste d'avoir rassemblé des données traditionnelles éparses dans la littérature antérieure et contemporaine, et de les avoir appliquées avec discernement au problème délicat qui l'occupait.'[37]

Two final points about sources call for brief comment. Jean Rivière has worked out very thoroughly the place of St. Bernard in this controversy, demonstrating how the celebrated *De consideratione* was invoked by the opposing sides.[38] Boniface VIII in *Unam sanctam* and his champions in their treatises used the great authority to enunciate the doctrine of the two swords. Their opponents, not least John of Paris, had recourse to St. Bernard to demonstrate that jurisdiction in temporal affairs was contrary to the mission entrusted to the papacy: *Forma apostolica haec est: dominatio interdicitur, indicitur ministerium.* John of Paris made this one of the main themes of his treatise. It was particularly in chapter 10, however, that he expounded the argument in its fulness, integrated with scriptural and

---

[37] *Op. cit.* 37.
[38] Rivière, *op. cit.* 403-23.

canonical arguments, to establish that Christ had given no power to St. Peter over lay property:

> These things have kings and princes as their judges. Why do you trespass on alien territory? Not because you are unworthy, but because it is an unworthy thing for you to concern yourselves with such matters, when you ought rather to be concerned with greater matters.

The final observation about sources concerns the origins of John of Paris' collection of forty-two arguments in favour of a papal power in temporal affairs. Some are identified by the author himself: two (nos. 20, 26) are Hugh of St. Victor's and two more may be confidently ascribed to the same source (nos. 21, 22); one (no. 30) is named as St. Bernard's; five (nos. 31, 38-41) are ascribed to the contemporary canonist Henry of Cremona who had written an unimpressive *De potestate papae*.[39] Nos. 1-19 are of canonist origin as the citations of canons and decretals shows. All these theses can be found cited or accepted in the work of Hostiensis, whom John of Paris quotes by name elsewhere. Two others (nos. 36, 37) seem also to have a specifically canonist (decretist) source. This leaves eleven remaining unidentified. It is to be remembered that John of Paris said expressly that he had assembled arguments he had heard as well as read.[40]

It is generally agreed among the commentators on the treatise that Aegidius Romanus was John of Paris' principal adversary and that he knew a substantial number of these papalist theses from his *On ecclesiastical power*. Both

---

[39] Edited by R. Scholz, *op. cit.* 459-516.
[40] "Hec sunt que audire vel colligere potui ad hanc partem".

modern editors of the treatise are of this opinion and both advance lists of arguments, somewhat different in make-up, attributed to the celebrated Augustinian. The attribution, however, is very doubtful. Neither of these treatises can be dated precisely; it is very probable they were being written contemporaneously. When the acid test is applied, and detailed comparison is made between the theses and the treatise, in no case is textual correlationship direct enough to make it certain that John had read *On ecclesiastical power*. There are resemblances — Aegidius Romanus quoted extensively from Hugh of St. Victor and St. Bernard — but no really convincing proof can be offered that John of Paris had knowledge of Aegidius Romanus' work. The same can be said too of James of Viterbo's *On Christian government* whose influence some have thought detectable.

There is one further feature calling for attention in any examination of the general make-up of *On royal and papal power*. John of Paris did not merely criticize individual papal theses. His attack was more radical. For he attempted a criticism of the methods by which they had formulated their arguments. He sought to cut them off at source.

It is not unexpected that John's methodology at its most characteristic is best revealed when he handled his main source, the Bible. His concern was to prune away exegetical accretions, to restore texts, which had been pressed into hierocratic service, to their traditional meanings. His aim was to close the credibility gap between what Scripture really said and what contemporary papal champions made of Scripture. This he did by taking his stand on the 'reading of the Saints' that is, on the interpretations of those like Augustine and Jerome whose commentary commanded all the respect of accepted tradition. In this way, such texts, so cherished by the hierocrats, as Jer. 1. 10 ('Lo, I have this day set thee over the nations ...'), 1 Cor. 6. 3 ('Do you not know you are to judge angels? ...'), Gen. 1.16 ('And God made two great lights') 1 Cor. 2. 15 ('But the spiritual man judgeth all things ...') were stripped of their political relevance by being put firmly back into their rightful context.

Closely allied to this successful principle of criticism, return to traditional exegesis, was his approach to arguments based on scriptural allegories. This can be best demonstrated by the example of the very important 'two swords' text (Luke 22. 38). It will be recalled that interpretations were current among papal writers which read this text either as giving the spiritual power authority to command the service of the temporal power at will or, more drastically, as an argument that secular power had its source in the spiritual power.

There were three elements in John of Paris' critique of this and similar arguments. Firstly, and most importantly, he applied a principle of methodology which originated with Augustine and (Pseudo) Denis the Areopagite: the mystical sense of Scripture, allegorical interpretation, would not of itself suffice to establish any proposition, unless it could be substantiated by a non-mystical, non-allegorical authority. Since John considered such authority was lacking in this case, there could be no force in the argument that the text established that Christ conferred both spiritual and temporal power on Peter, and hence on the pope. The second line of criticism was this: let it be granted that the text might be read in the mystical sense, as indeed it had been so read in the past very frequently, yet 'none of the Saints whose teaching is approved and confirmed by the

Church' had read it as a political allegory. There were a number of traditional authoritative mystical readings available, but none of them understood the text as referring to spiritual and temporal powers. Again, third element of the critique, let it be granted that the allegory was intended as a political one. Nevertheless, it cannot be established that it should be read as implying the derivation of temporal from spiritual authority. For Peter had not been given two swords; other texts could be adduced to show that Peter had but the one sword from Christ, the spiritual. As for the temporal sword, permission to use it had been granted to the spiritual power but that should be only by the consent and authority of its legal holder, the secular ruler. Churchmen, in other words, could not compel the use of the temporal sword, only request that it be used.

John of Paris applied other principles of source criticism. One, which he shared with the *Quaestio in utramque partem,* concerned the admissibility of evidence from papal sources in favour of the papacy's own position. When the issue in debate was papal power in temporal affairs, what a text from an imperial source said in the papacy's favour carried authority. But evidence for the pope from a papal source was only of weight if it were confirmed by Scripture. In other words, a pope was an unreliable witness in his own cause unless his evidence was substantiated otherwise. A case in point concerned a statement which Gratian had attributed to Nicholas I (it was actually St. Peter Damian's) that Christ had conferred 'rights of both heavenly and earthly empires'. With his habitual recourse to the Saints, John of Paris was able to show that there was no scriptural authority for any reading of Matthew 16.

18 which gave Peter power over any earthly empire in any literal sense.

There was one last methodological lesson which John of Paris wished to bring home to papalists: history was a double-edged weapon. For they were prone to over-generalize from historical particularities. Thus they deduced from events like the participation of Pope Zachary in the removal of Childeric III, the last Merovingian king, and the alleged translation of the Empire from the Greeks to Charlemagne, that the pope had power to depose rulers and translate empires. John of Paris pointed out the pit-falls of deducing general principles of law from events which were of their nature unique, the product of a special set of circumstances. For there were numerous examples to be found in history where it had been the temporal power which had been exercising authority in ecclesiastical affairs. If these particular events were likewise to be generalized, it would have to be accepted, for example, that it was for the emperor to transfer the primacy of churches or to establish their precedence or that no pope might be elected without the emperor's consent. Clearly, no pope would accept such propositions. Legal principles then, should not be deduced from the historical accidents of the distant past.

V. THE GENERAL ARGUMENT

The *On royal and papal power* is a relatively short piece of writing, its architecture is coherent and logical, its style, within its convention, lucid, its line of argument direct and uncluttered. No elaborate analysis of its general argument is called for: *Joannes optimus sui interpres.* Nevertheless some interpretative observations may be offered by way of introduction to a reading of the text itself.

Reflecting on the course of the quarrel between Boniface VIII and Philip IV, on the official diplomatic exchanges, treatises, pamphlets and orations it occasioned, one issue can be seen standing out as crucial for each of the two sides: the mutual threat of deposition. Could a king of France be deposed by a pope, as Boniface had so loftily and threateningly asserted he could be? Could a pope be put on trial and himself be deposed, as the French came to assert in their turn? No doubt the final answers to these questions lay in *de facto* situations where force rather than political theories tended to decide political problems. But arbitrariness was not all. Each side could argue that the law was on its side and muster a legal justification of some respectability. The importance of John of Paris' treatise lies in his recognition of that fact and that he was the only contemporary political theorist who considered each of these cases in detail. The examination of deposing powers, papal and royal, formed the axis of his treatise. Round this theme revolved the other basic questions he was concerned to analyse: the origins and ends of the spiritual and temporal powers and the harmonious integration of their respective functions. The question of removing individuals from political and ecclesiastical office was integrally connected with the origins of political and ecclesiastical power. To ask questions about the breaking of kings and popes is necessarily to ask questions about their making. Hence John of Paris was inevitably led into considering all the fundamental questions of the origin and purposes of both temporal and spiritual powers.

It had long been an accepted part of papal political
thinking that emperors could be deposed. Nor was this
mere theory. The actions of Gregory VII against Henry IV
and of Innocent IV against Frederick II had demonstrated
that there was more to the claim than the speculations of
academics. Canonists had no doubts about the deposition
logic, especially after the First Council of Lyons, where,
in 1245, the arguments for a papal deposing power having
been thoroughly ventilated by the Council Fathers, Frederick II had been deposed. It can be seen stated compre-
hensively in the work of Hostiensis, himself a participant
in the Lyons council.[41]

There were a number of phases in the argument. It
rested ultimately on a particular reading of Scripture. The
commission of the keys as stated in Matthew 16. 19 and
as prefigured in Jeremias 1. 10 provided the fundamental
justification. Deposition was essentially an extension of
excommunication. The power of the keys gave to the
pope the authority of binding and loosing on earth, of
ejecting and admitting individuals, then, from and into
the congregation of the faithful. No person, however
eminent, was exempt from this juridiction, no moral matter
beyond its scope. A ruler could be excommunicated if he
did wrong. If he persisted in his wrongful conduct, thereby
showing himself incorrigible, he was deemed unfit to rule
in a Christian society. He was so declared and his subjects
released from their obligations of civil obedience.

Popes and canonists were the quicker to make this ex-

---

[41] Cf. my "Medieval Deposition Theory: A Neglected Canonist *Consultatio*
from the First Council of Lyons," *Studies in Church History* 2 (ed. G. J. Cuming
1965) 197-214.

tension of the excommunication penalty because of the special relationship that existed between the papacy and the empire. The emperor had his election confirmed by the pope, was crowned by him and swore an oath to him. Logic seemed to demand that if confirmation of an election and of a candidate was to be anything more than a formality, the pope had power to judge the legality of an imperial election, to exclude an unsatisfactory candidate, even to arbitrate and make the final choice in cases of double election. The justification for this papal authority lay in history, in the alleged translation of the Empire from Greeks to Romans in the famous ceremony of Christmas Day 800 when Charlemagne was papally created Roman Emperor. The Translation was the living example of the principle that it was for the pope to decide who was or who was not suitable to be emperor.

There was another historical argument with which popes and canonists made great play. Boniface VIII himself made specific reference to it when claiming his predecessors had deposed three French kings in the past. This was the alleged deposition of Childeric III, the last Merovingian king, by Pope Zachary I, and the consequent substitution of Peppin, father of Charlemagne. The important deductions here were that firstly, this was an example of deposition which concerned a king who had no special constitutional relationship to the pope. In other words, kings other than emperors might also be deposed. Further, Childeric was deposed for inefficiency or inadequacy, not for sin. He lost his throne not *ratione peccati* but simply because (it was argued) the pope decided he was not up to his job.

The key to the demolition of this logic lay simply in the demonstration that the power given by Christ to the priest-

hood was such as to preclude any possibility of it exercising
coercive power over rulers. Ministers of the Gospel were
commissioned to preach the kingdom of God: 'They lead
the rest to a share in the heavenly kingdom not only
through the force of their love but also by virtue of their
function of teaching and of administering the sacraments'.
This charge had nothing to do with exercising jurisdiction
over rulers. John's central argument, powerfully and convincingly urged, was that the work of the 'sacred ones'
(*sacerdotes*) was confined exclusively to the sacral order,
of which, mediators in spiritual things between God and
man, they were the appointed leaders and directors: 'The
priesthood is that spiritual power given by Christ to the
ministers of his Church of administering the sacraments to
the faithful'. The sum of priestly rule over the community
of the faithful lay in three acts: 'illumination through
doctrine, purification through correction, perfection through
the sacraments'. Nothing of temporal lordship or jurisdiction had been given with these powers.[42]

There were three main lines of proof which John of
Paris pursued with some fair measure of elaboration to
establish that the priesthood did not have coercive power
over princes.

The first proof concerned the kingship of Christ.[43]
Priests were appointed to lead men into the kingdom of
Christ. Christ's kingdom, however, on his own explicit
profession, was not of this world and those, who thought it
was, like Herod, even for long the Apostles themselves and
now 'certain moderns', erred grievously. Christ on earth did

---

[42] Chapters 2, 12, 13 are the specially relevant ones with chapt. 13 perhaps
the most important in the treatise.

[43] Chapters 2 and especially 8 contain his doctrine.

not exercise lordship and jurisdiction. 'He whose days are for eternity' was not a temporal king.

The second proof concerned Christ's charge to his Apostles. Even if Christ had exercised such jurisdiction he most assuredly had not commissioned his Apostles to exercise it. John of Paris' detailed examination of this proposition stands epitomized in St. Bernard's exegesis of Luke 12.13-15: 'It cannot be shown that any of the Apostles ever sat as judge of men or as an adjudicator of boundaries or as a distributor of lands. I read that the Apostles had to stand as men under accusation; I do not read that they sat as accusers'.

The third proof concerned the nature of the authority that had been given to secular rulers. Power had been conferred on these, 'God's ministers', immediately from God and therefore not mediately through the Church or pope. Though their sphere of action lay in the temporal and the corporal, the purpose of secular government was moral: the common good of the citizens, where the good is understood as life according to virtue. The origins of political authority lay, after God, in natural law and the law of nations. It had been established before the priesthood, hence it did not need clerical authorization to give it validity:

> Royal power existed in its own right in both principle and practice before papal power, and there were kings before there were Christians in France. Therefore in neither principle nor practice is the royal power there from the pope but from God and the people who choose a king either as an individual or as a member of a dynasty, as was in fact done formerly.[44]

[44] Cf. Chapter 10.

Thus John of Paris achieved a theory of dualism of the powers, pressing into service different strands of political thinking, old and new. There was, firstly, an older ecclesiastical tradition, rooted in scriptural exegesis, and still to be found in the canon law, which saw the powers as distinct and coordinate because the temporal power originated directly in God. Then there was another tradition, characteristic of Roman thinking, on the will of the people as the source of rulership. Finally came the Aristotelian emphasis on the rational and moral in the origin and purposes of civil government.

It followed from this dualism that there must be some other explanation of the papal role in the deposition of Childeric from the Frankish kingship and the promotion of Charlemagne to the Roman emperorship than that offered by orthodox papal theory. John of Paris could propound several different interpretations. He looked to other historical sources and read the historical record differently (and in the case of Childeric, much nearer to historical truth). He rejected the whole method, as has been seen, of generalizing from particular *de facto* situations. But, most significantly, he rejected the deposition and translation theories on the grounds that it was for civil society itself to do the deposing or the translating: power to depose Childeric lay with the Frankish barons, the translation of the empire required the consent of the people, which was the constitutive act in the transfer. Political authority was vested in the community and it alone had power to make new dispositions about rulership.

It is to be noticed that John of Paris did not reject the notion that a king might be deposed. Clearly, he regarded monarchy as limited by duty to the community, an office to be exercised in accordance with the common good. John was not in this treatise concerned primarily with the mis-deeds of kings and the abuse of the temporal power. Hence this theme of the limitation of royal power was muted. The same logic applied analogously to papal power was, however, amply ventilated.

That the apostolic see might judge all and itself be judged by no human authority was a venerable papal legal axiom, and numerous canons in the *Decretum* testified to this fact. But John of Paris was able to turn to the *Decretum* to exploit another line of thought he found there which made a significant exception to the principle of papal immunity. Thereby was opened up the possibility of building a case for papal deposition on established legal principles. *Dist.* 40 c. 6 (*Si papa*) stated:

> No human shall presume to convict the pope of faults of this nature because he who must judge all is judged by no one, unless he is discovered to be errant in faith.

This text with its last significant if ambiguous *nisi deprehendatur a fide deuius* clause was like every other canon in the *Decretum* extensively glossed by successive gene-rations of canonists. The principle that a pope might be judged for heresy was not called into serious question. In-deed, so stalwart a papal champion as Pope Innocent III himself stated more than once his acceptance of the general principle.[45] *Si papa* did suggest problems to canonists how-

---

[45] In his *Sermones in consecratione pontificis* PL 217.657, 664, 670. Cf. especially: "Propter causam vero fornicationis Ecclesia Romana posset dimittere Romanum pontificem. Fornicationem non dico carnalem, sed spiritualem: quia non est carnale, sed spirituale coniugium, id est, propter infidelitatis errorem, quoniam qui non credit iam iudicatus est (John 3.18)" *ibid.* 664. In the context, "Romana Ecclesia" might mean either the universal Church or the College of Cardinals.

ever, of which the two most important were: could a pope be accused of crimes other than heresy? how, regarding the matter procedurally, was a pope to be brought to judgment?

On the first of these questions, opinion among canonists varied. But the most important decretist of the twelfth century, Huguccio, argued powerfully that a pope could be condemned for any notorious crime if, after admonition, he were unwilling to reform.[46] This view was reflected in the *glossa ordinaria* on the *Decretum* where Joannes Teutonicus repeated the gist of what Huguccio had said and committed himself to the opinion:

> Certainly I believe that if his crime is notorious and thereby is a source of scandal to the universal Church, and if he is incorrigible, then he can be accused.

Joannes Teutonicus did not say in so many words that once condemned the pope should be deposed. But John of Paris was not to leave any i's undotted or t's uncrossed. A pope might be deposed if he were an incorrigible heretic, a cause of scandal, guilty of some serious crime, had abused his stewardship of ecclesiastical property, right of which was vested in the whole ecclesiastical community, or, being incapacitated, refused to resign. In short, he might be deposed if the exercise of his authority was against the common good.[47]

---

[46] Cf. V. Martin, "Comment s'est formée la doctrine de la supériorité du concile sur le pape. 1. La tradition canonique avant le grand schisme d'occident," *Revue des sciences religieuses* 17 (1937) 121-43. For a translation of Huguccio's gloss and also of one by Alanus Anglicus which would almost certainly be closer than Huguccio to Innocent III's point of view, Tierney, *Crisis of Church and State*, 124-6.

[47] The topic of papal deposition occurs in chapters 6, 13, 22, 24, 25.

The *glossa ordinaria* itself had nothing specific to say as to the practicalities of accusation, trial, penalties. Effectively, there could be only two agents. Most often favoured was a General Council, recourse to which being always accepted among canonists as normal procedure in any emergency situation affecting the whole Church. The College of Cardinals was also occasionally mentioned in this context. Either way, the principle was the same: judgment was to be by the whole Church as represented either in a General Council or in the College of Cardinals. John of Paris on at least four occasions in the treatise expressed his confidence in the College of Cardinals acting *in loco ecclesiae* as the appropriate instrument of deposition.

The reasoning behind this view is crucial for the understanding of John's ecclesiology:

> I believe however that the College of Cardinals on its own is adequate to depose, for it would seem that the body whose consent, *in place of the whole Church*, makes a pope, might conversely, unmake him.

The pope then is created by the whole Church. He is to rule for the whole Church, 'for building up, not for destruction':

> No one is chosen to be pope for any reason other than the common good of the Church and the Lord's flock. The end of his ruling activity is the common benefit.[48]

John emphatically rejected any notion that papal will of itself conferred legality on a papal act, even if the action were contrary to law. If he acted against the common good,

[48] Cf. chapt. 24.

he was accountable to the whole Church. Further, his rule should be with the whole Church. John of Paris envisaged the constitution of the Church as mixed, containing monarchical, aristocratic and democratic elements, and concluded:

> It would certainly be the best constitution for the Church if under the one pope, many were chosen by and from each province, so that all would participate in some way in the government of the Church.[49]

John of Paris, who accepted that the pope had plenitude of power, was attempting to combine this principle of papal sovereignty with the principle of communal sovereignty. He here sounded a note with a peculiarly modern ring about it.

There is one last dimension to John of Paris' deposition theory which throws light on his general theory of the relations of the powers. It has been seen that his primary postulate was a principle of dualism, of distinct, coordinate powers. In the event, however, there were limits to John of Paris' dualism. In the final analysis he was not prepared to make a complete divorce between the respective spheres of action. For although he ruled out the direct exercise of the authority of the one power in the sphere of the other, he did not preclude an indirect effect of the one on the other. A pope might play a part in the deposing of a king; an emperor or a king might take a hand in the deposition of a pope.

Given his French loyalties and the atmosphere of the period when he was writing, it is perhaps not surprising

---

[49] Cf. chapt. 19.

that John of Paris allowed a lay ruler considerable scope for action against a pope. But he also allowed a pope at least as much and possibly more scope for action against a lay ruler. Each was to have an indirect or 'incidental' power to act against the other in certain emergency situations. If a pope through abuse of the spiritual sword (such as pronouncing anyone a heretic who denied that the king of France was subject to him temporally) had created danger of rebellion, the king might defend himself and his country by using his influence to bring about the pope's excommunication and deposition. He might also inflict penalties on those of his subjects who persisted in obedience to such a pope. On the other hand, if a ruler were an incorrigible heretic, paying no heed to his excommunication, the pope might initiate such action as would lead to his deposition by his people — by excommunicating all who continued to obey him, for example. Thus each could take action against the other even though one has only spiritual jurisdiction and the other only temporal jurisdiction.[50] In the last analysis, then, John of Paris went for the compromise. He had done much to prune the idea of spiritual power of its illegitimate political accretions. He had still left it, however, with a powerful political weapon.

VI. APPRAISAL

It is easy to understand why the Gallicans so appreciated John of Paris. The fundamental theses of his treatise were

[50] The "incidental" power of each to unseat the other is discussed in chapter 13.

exactly in accord with the first of the Four Gallican Articles of 1682, namely that the power conferred on Peter and his successors was over the spiritual matters of the Church and those which pertained to eternal salvation and not over civil and temporal matters, with the concomitant rejection of a papal deposing power or right to release subjects from their obligations of obedience to the civil power. There was too, in the treatise, an 'evident anticipation' of the Conciliar movement, as well as a concern to uphold the rules, customs and institutions of the French Church, which were in accord with the principles of the second and third of the Articles. Finally, when John of Paris' view of the papal *magisterium,* or power to make decisions about the faith, is examined in detail, it will be found to be along lines similar to the principle succinctly summarized in the fourth and final article of the Gallican Declaration. This was the principle which, while conceding the power of decision to the pope, hedged it with the qualification that his judgment was not unchangeable unless it received the general assent of the whole Church.[51]

It is abundantly clear then, that John of Paris was no thorough-going papalist. But just how anti-papal was he? Or, putting the question another way, was he a critic of the papacy in the fashion of the revolutionary Marsilius of Padua? It can certainly be agreed that there are some similarities and anticipations of the *Defensor Pacis.* John

---

[51] Cf. S. Z. Ehler and J. B. Morrall, *Church and State through the Centuries* (1954) 205-208. On John of Paris as one whose "work in fact provides by far the most consistent and complete formulation of conciliar doctrine before the outbreak of the Great Schism" see B. Tierney, *Foundations of the Conciliar Theory* (Cambridge 1955) 157-78.

of Paris showed Marsilius' hostility to the exercise of co-ercive power by priests over lay rulers, his urge to rethink from their first principles such topics as the nature of the priesthood and the nature of the power wielded by Christ and the Apostles, his emphasis on the *populus* in the exercise of power and the responsibility of both lay and ecclesiastical rulers to it. In essence, however, the similarity is superficial. For what made Marsilius revolutionary was his rejection of any divinely granted papal primacy over the universal Church. According to Marsilius, Christ had not commanded Peter to be superior to the other Apostles; there was no Petrine succession, no vicariate of Christ, no plenitude of power. If any especial authority had been granted to the bishop of Rome it had come merely from human authority, not divine command. In short, papal primacy, in so far as it existed at all, was an historical accident, and was exercised only for reasons of admini-strative convenience and because the civil power permitted it.[52]

A simple textual comparison establishes the width of the gulf between the two. Here is Marsilius' position on the primacy in a nutshell:

> And when it is added that the church is one only through the numerical unity of some bishop who is superior to the others, I deny this; and even if I were to grant it, I would deny the other inference which sought to prove that the Roman bishop has been made such head or leader of the church immediately through divine ordainment... Moreover, the Roman bishop is not by God's immediate ordainment the particular successor of

[52] *Defensor Pacis* esp. Discourse II chaps. 15-16, 22-25.

St. Peter or of any other apostle in such a way that superior authority over the bishops belongs to him because of this ... but rather, if he does have any special authority, it belongs to him through human appointment or election...[53]

As compared with this total rejection of the primacy, John of Paris remained firmly orthodox:

It is obvious that despite the fact that peoples are divided into different dioceses and communities where bishops rule in spiritual matters, there is yet one church of all the faithful forming one Christian people. Just as in each diocese there is one bishop who is the head of the church of the people there, so in the whole church and Christian people as a whole there is one supreme head, the Roman pope, successor of Peter. For the church militant is fashioned on the model of the church triumphant which has one head presiding over the whole universe. Hence the Apocalypse: 'And they shall be his people and God himself with them shall be their God'; and Osea: 'And the children of Juda shall be gathered together: and they shall appoint themselves one head and shall come up out of the land'. Hence also John: 'They shall be one fold and one shepherd'; this text cannot be interpreted as referring only to Christ; it speaks of some one minister ruling everyone in his place. For with the removal of Christ's physical presence it happens on oc-casion that there are difficulties about the faith, and then diversity of opinion would divide the Church, whose unity demands unity of belief, unless there were some simple authoritative decision through which the unity of the church might be preserved. The one who holds this pre-eminence is Peter and his successor. He does not

---

[53] *Defensor Pacis* II.28.13. The translation is that of A. Gewirth, *op. cit.* 2.383.

hold his position because of some decree of a council. He holds it from the very mouth of the Lord himself who, before his ascension, being unwilling to leave his church in any way lacking in anything essential to it, gave this charge to Peter alone: 'Feed my sheep': and before his passion he had said already: 'Thou being once converted confirm thy brethren'.[54]

and again:

It is this jurisdiction or supreme prelacy over the whole Church which was given to Peter, by subjecting the faithful to him, when he was told 'Feed my sheep', that is, 'Be shepherd and prelate, and I commit and subject the Church to you as shepherd'. Thus Theophilus: 'The meal over, he committed the care of the sheep to Peter and to no other person'. Gregory says very much the same. So, therefore, although all the Apostles received the same equal power of the keys and jurisdiction from Christ, yet it was Peter alone, and whoever on whom he wished to confer it, who received the power of jurisdiction and its subject matter. In this reading 'Feed my sheep' does not mean that the supreme power of determining jurisdiction had been given to Peter, though originally it had been held by all the Apostles, but that jurisdiction was given in the first place to Peter alone and afterwards he distributed it in parts, calling others to a share of the pastoral charge.[55]

In the light of these views, it is not surprising to find John of Paris using the term 'plenitude of power' to

[54] Chapt. 3, pp. 84-5.

[55] Chapt. 12, pp. 147-8. Cf. also : "Nevertheless the pope can be cescribed also as head of the church as to the hierarchy of ministers, in that he is the chief minister, from whom, as from the principal vicar of Christ in spirituel matters, the whole order of ministers depends, as from its summit and its foundation, inasmuch as the Roman Church is unquestionably head of all the churches", chapter 18.

describe papal authority in the Church.[56] It was this very
term which Marsilius wrote his treatise to discredit.

John of Paris was really much more of a traditionalist
than a radical. His ecclesiology, centring on a thoroughly
orthodox interpretation of the primacy, was traditional
enough. Even his trenchant views about deposing a pope
were more acceptable in official circles than modern commentators have sometimes been prepared to concede.[57]
Concerning the two powers, he was again essentially traditional. For his view of the dualism of the powers was
in essence but the rationale of the sovereign position
which the king of France actually had held in the past
and was to continue to hold in the future, a position
which the popes themselves had certainly tolerated, even encouraged and against which, after the clash, they were to attempt little in the way of change. A French king was in truth
souverain es choses temporieux and a living embodiment of
the maxim *rex in regno suo est imperator,* independent alike
of pope, as far as temporal affairs were concerned, and of the
emperor. Further, he enjoyed certain privileges in eccle-

[56] Chapt. 6.

[57] Innocent III's view is relevant here (n. 45 above). Especially significant
in this context is an opinion put to John XXII by one of his professional theologians. Consulted by the Pope about the errors of Marsilius of Padua, the
Carmelite Sybert of Beek told him that an emperor might only intervene in the
deposition of a pope when asked to do so by the Church or by the College of
Cardinals. And this applied in cases of notorious crime as well as heresy:
"In secundo vero casu reputo, quod imperator se intromittere non deberet,
nisi ab ecclesia seu a cetu cardinalium esset requisitus; et haberet forte hoc
non solum locum in heresi, sed etiam in omni notorio crimine, si inde scanda-
lizetur ecclesia et papa incorrigibilis esset, prout notatur di. XL *Si papa*, et
sic invenitur in cronicis aliquando fuisse factum." *Reprobatio sex errorum* ed.
R. Scholz, *Unbekannte kirchenpolitische Streitschriften aus der Zeit Ludwigs des
Bayern (1327-1354)* 2 (Rome 1914) 11. It is difficult to see any difference
between this view of a papal adviser and John of Paris's.

siastical matters, most notably in rights of collation and presentation. What John of Paris did in his treatise was to establish that this traditional *de facto* independence could be vindicated *de iure*. This he set out to do, with a high degree of success in the attempt, by recourse to traditions of another sort: the exegetical tradition of the early church wherein the Scriptures demonstrated the principles of a dualistic view of politics, and its juridical tradition which demonstrated its practice in the history of the church.

This view of the over-all traditionalism of the *On royal and papal power* gives John of Paris his place in the history of political thought. He was the first to provide a systematic demonstration that the political traditions and practices of a national kingdom had their fundamental justification in divine, natural and ecclesiastical law. It was a justification which the papacy had long, for the most part, implicitly acknowledged.

TEXT

ON ROYAL AND PAPAL POWER

PROEMIUM

From time to time it happens that while trying to avoid one false position we fall into its exact opposite one. For example there are people who maintain according to the *Decretum,*[1] that because monks are dead to the world they should not administer the sacraments of penance and baptism since to do this is alien to the spirit of monasticism. Others, wishing to avoid this error or perhaps to anticipate it, have argued that it is precisely because of their call to the highest state that they might hear confessions, absolve and inflict remedial penances. Sound doctrine lies between these errors. The monastic state neither specially fits nor unfits them for public ministration of the sacraments. They may do so however if their bishops, to whom ordinary jurisdiction in this respect belongs, authorize them to do so.

We can see another example of truth occupying a middle position between two opposing errors in the book *Concerning the Two Natures and One Person of Christ.*[2] It is shown there that orthodoxy lies between the error of Nestorius on the one side and of Eutyches on the other.

It is in similar fashion that the truth about sacerdotal power can be found in the middle position between two erroneous opinions. On the one hand, the Waldensians have erred with their assertion that the successors of the Apostles, namely the pope and ecclesiastical hierarchy,

---

[1] *Decretum Gratiani* 16 q. 1 c. 8.
[2] Boethius, *Liber de persona et duabus naturis.* PL 64.1341.

were denied any power in temporal affairs and that it was unlawful for them to possess temporal wealth. They go on to argue that the true church of God with genuine apostolic succession in its prelates endured only until Pope Sylvester's time. For when the church accepted Constantine's donation it became Roman and no longer the true church of God. In their view the true church has been eclipsed except in so far as it is preserved and restored by themselves.

Among the arguments they put forward to justify their case are the following texts of Scripture:

'Lay not up to yourselves treasures on earth.'[3]
'But having food and wherewith to be covered, with these we are content. For they that will become rich' etc.[4]
'You cannot serve God and mammon.'[5]
'Be not solicitous therefore saying, what shall we eat...'[6]
'Behold the birds of the air for they neither sow nor do they reap.'[7]
'Do not possess gold nor silver nor money in your purses.'[8]
'So likewise everyone of you that doth not renounce all he possesseth...'[9]
'Silver and gold have I none.'[10]

It is to such evidence that they look for proof for the opinion that the prelates of the Church of God as successors of the Apostles should have no claim to temporal wealth.

[3] Matth. 6.19.
[4] 1 Tim. 6.8, 9.
[5] Matth. 6.24.
[6] Matth. 6.34.
[7] Matth. 6.26.
[8] Matth. 10.9.
[9] Luke 14.33.
[10] Acts 3.6.

On the other hand, standing opposed to the Waldensian error is the position of Herod who on learning of the birth of a king called Christ believed that his kingship was of the human kind. Certain moderns seem to have taken their views from this source. For they have moved so far from the first error as to assert that the pope, in so far as he stands in Christ's place on earth has a power over the properties of princes and barons as well as cognizance and jurisdiction of them. They say that the pope has power in temporalities in a more excellent way than the prince because he has primary authority, derived directly from God, whereas the prince has his power mediately from God through the pope. They go on to argue that the pope only exercises this power in certain determined cases, as the decretal *Per venerabilem* states.[11] It is the prince who has the immediate executive power. Anyone who has spoken differently has in their view taken the part of the princes. If the pope sometimes says that he has no temporal jurisdiction, this must be understood as referring to regular and immediate exercise of jurisdiction, or because he wants to maintain peace between church and princes or to ensure that prelates are not overprone to become preoccupied with temporal matters and secular business. They argue further that the relationship of the pope to temporalities is different in kind from that of princes and prelates. For he is sole true lord in that he can at will absolve a usurer from the debt he owes through his crime, take from another as he wishes what otherwise belongs to him, and that should he do such an act it is valid, even though he commits sin in doing it, though he should only do it

[11] *Decretales* 4.17.13.

for such reasonable cause as defence of the church or the like. Other prelates and princes, by contrast, are not lords but guardians, agents, stewards.

This opinion concerning lordship of property has also a source besides Herod's error. It seems to continue the misconception of Vigilantius. Everyone believes and must believe that nothing pertaining to evangelical perfection is repugnant to the status of pope. But it is clear that if the pope, by reason of his status as pope and vicar of Christ, is lord of all, renunciation of property right and of lord-ship in temporal affairs must be considered repugnant to his papal status, since it is quite contrary to what is appropriate for his state. Hence, as Vigilantius argued, poverty and rejection of temporal lordship does not pertain to evangelical perfection. About this Augustine wrote in his *On the Christian Combat*[12] that there were some who seek only their own advantage, Catholics though they were, and look for their own glory in the name of Christ, as if they were heretics. Among these heretics there arose of old in Gaul previously free of such monstrosities one Vigilantius[13] to be numbered among those who equated the state of riches with that of poverty, just as at an earlier time Jovinian in Italy seems to have thought marriage superior to chastity.[14] Moreover this opinion about property has something of that arrogance of the Pharisees who taught the people that they need not pay taxes to Caesar since they gave tithe and offerings to God so that, as Jerome says, they might obtain more for themselves from

---

[12] Cf. *De agone christiano* c.10 PL 40.297.
[13] Cf. *Adversus Vigilantium* 1, c.13 PL 23.365.
[14] Cf. Jerome, *Adversus Iovinianum* 1.3 PL 23.223.

those who had been made richer by being released from their other obligations. Furthermore this opinion seems dangerous for it means that when converts to the faith are made their rights over their own property are transferred to the pope. Thus the faith is made to appear less appealing to them and they draw back from it since through it the rights proper to their status are disrupted, as the gloss on 1 Peter 2 states. It must be said of this opinion that it arouses the fear that, in the words of Chrysostom in his commentary on Matthew,[15] while business deals are being made in the house of God, Christ may appear in angry severity to cleanse his temple with a whip and to turn a den of thieves into a house of prayer.

As between these antithetical views (everyone would agree that the first is false) truth lies midway. Against the first opinion, it must be believed that it is not wrong for prelates to have lordship and jurisdiction in temporalities. But this power is not theirs because of what they are or because they are vicars of Christ and successors of the Apostles. It can be quite appropriate for them to have such in virtue of the concession and permission of rulers if they are so endowed through the piety of rulers or receive them from some other source.

I make solemn declaration that in nothing I assert do I purpose anything against faith, good morals or sound doctrine, or against the reverence due to the person or office of pope. Should anything detrimental to any of these be found in my book either directly or indirectly I wish it to be withdrawn and I want it to be understood that this

---

[15] *Opus imperfectum in Matthaeum homil.* 38 PG 56.841.

declaration applies to each and every individual argument I advance.

The matter I have proposed for examination is discussed in the following order of chapters:

In the first is shown what is the nature and origin of royal government.

In the second, the nature and origin of the priesthood.

In the third the ordering of ministers to one supreme head is discussed and it is argued that there is not the same need for a hierarchical ordering of secular rulers under a supreme head as there is for ministers of the church to be so ordered.

In the fourth there is examination of which came first in time, kingship or priesthood.

In the fifth which comes first in dignity is considered.

In the sixth, it is proved that the priesthood is not first in an order of causality. First it is shown in what way the pope has power over church property.

In the seventh papal power over lay property is analyzed.

In the eighth it is proved that the pope derives no jurisdiction from Christ over the property of laymen because Christ himself did not have such jurisdiction.

Chapter nine puts forward arguments for the contrary position, namely that Christ did have such jurisdiction, and replies to them.

Chapter ten argues that even if it were agreed that Christ did have such jurisdiction he did not commit it to Peter.

Chapter eleven lists the arguments to the contrary, namely that the pope has jurisdiction over temporal goods.

The twelfth chapter treats of some notions preliminary to the refutation of the arguments of the preceding chapter and to the proper understanding of what authority Christ has given the pope in regard to temporalities. In the first place the powers given by Christ to Peter and the Apostles is discussed and in the next chapter, thirteen, it is proved that prelates do not have lordship or jurisdiction in temporalities because of these powers nor are princes subject to prelates in temporalities because of them.

Chapter fourteen is a reply to the first six arguments of the opposing case (as listed in chapter eleven) and the next six chapters each deals in turn with a further six arguments.

In chapter twenty-one the donation of Constantine is discussed and what the pope can do because of it is examined.

In chapter twenty-two there is a discussion of whether it is allowed to dispute and make judgments about questions concerning the pope.

Chapter twenty-three posits the trifling arguments of those who say that a pope cannot resign.

In chapter twenty-four it is demonstrated that he can do so and in chapter twenty-five the arguments to the contrary are refuted.

CHAPTER I

The nature and origin of royal government

When considering the nature of royal government the following definition of the correct sense of the word kingdom should be known: it is the government of a perfect or self-sufficient community by one man for the sake of the common good. In this definition 'government' is the genus: 'community' is added to differentiate it from government where each governs himself either by natural instinct, as is the case with animals, or by reason, as is the case with those who live a solitary life. 'Perfect' serves to distinguish the community from the family which is not self-sufficient for anything more than a short period of time and not for all the needs of life as is the community, as the Philosopher teaches in the first book of his *Politics*.[1] 'For the sake of the common good' is included in the definition to distinguish it from oligarchy, tyranny and democracy, in which the ruler seeks nothing but his own good, especially in a tyranny. 'By one man' is included to distinguish it from an aristocracy, that is the rule of the best men, where government in accordance with virtue is in the hands of a few. Some people call this sort of government rule according to the decisions of the prudent or of a senate. It is included also to distinguish it from a *polycratia* or rule of the many where the people rule by plebiscite. He who is not alone in his power is

[1] *Politics* 1.1-2.

not a king, as the Lord said through Ezekiel: 'My servant David shall be set over them and they shall all have one shepherd'.[2]

Government as defined above has its roots in natural law and the law of nations. For since man is by nature created a political and civil animal, as is said in Book 1 of the *Politics*[3] — the Philosopher deduces this from man's need for food, clothing and protection which man in isolation cannot supply for himself and from man's speech, the purpose of which is communication with others; these considerations apply to man only — he must of necessity live in a community and in such a community as is self-sufficient in all life's necessaries. The community of the family or of the village is not self-sufficient but the city-state or kingdom is, for in a single household or village are not to be found all those necessities of food, clothing and protection for a man's whole life as can be found in a city-state or kingdom. A society in which everyone seeks only his own advantage will collapse and disintegrate unless it is ordered to the good of all by some one ruler who has charge of the common good, just as a man's body would collapse if there were not in it some general force directing the common good of the members as a whole. Hence Solomon says in the Book of Proverbs: 'Where there is no governor the people shall fall'.[4] Such a governor is indeed a necessity, for what is particular to an individual is not the same as what is common to all. For men differ as to what is individual whereas what is common joins them together. There are different causes of different effects,

[2] Ezech. 34.23.
[3] *Politics* 1.2.
[4] Prov. 11.14.

so it is necessary that there should be provision made for the promotion of the common good in addition to that moving each individual to seek his own good.

Government of a community is more effective when conducted by one man according to virtue, than when exercised by many or few virtuous men. This is clear from the weighing-up of a number of points: firstly, considering power: virtue is more united and therefore the stronger in one ruler than when divided among many. Secondly, considering the unity and peace which rulers seek to provide for their communities: there can be no community where unity and concord is missing. But the single ruler better upholds that unity of a community which gives it its being than the rule of many; so therefore the rule of one man according to virtue will the better keep peace, and concord among citizens will not easily be broken. Thirdly, a single ruler has a sharper eye for the common good than many rulers can have even if they are ruling according to virtue. For the more who, as rulers, stand apart from the mass of the community, so the less do the remainder, the ruled, represent what is common, and vice versa. Hence the Philosopher says that among all the different types of constitution directed to the interest of those who rule, the tyrant is the worst because his object is his own advantage and not the advantage of those he governs.[5] Fourthly, in the law of nature all government is reduced to overall unity just as in any body composed of a mixture of parts there is one element which is master over the others. For example, in the heterogeneous human body, there is a principal member in the whole man and the soul contains all the elements. Animals which herd together and for

[5] Aristotle, *Nicomachean Ethics* 8.10.

whom it is natural to live in society are subject to one ruler.

From these arguments it is clear that it is both necessary and advantageous for man to live in society and especially in such a society as a city or kingdom which is self-sufficient in everything that pertains to the whole of life, and especially, too, under the government of one who rules the common good, who is called king. It is clear also that this sort of government derives from natural law in that man is a civil or political and social animal. Before the time of Belus and Ninus, who were the first to exercise government, men did not live as men according to what was proper to their nature but rather as did the beasts, without rule, as Orosius describes how some men lived in the first book of his *Against the Pagans*.[6] Cicero also describes something similar in the beginning of his *Vetus Rhetorica*,[7] while in the *Politics*, the Philosopher speaks of those who live like gods or beasts and not like men.[8] Since these men could not by the use of the speech common to all men bring themselves to live the common life natural to them, and to abandon a state more fitting for beasts than men, others, moved by the situation of these men in their error, and using their reason to better effect, tried to bring them by more persuasive arguments to an ordered life in common under one ruler, as Cicero says. Once thus brought together, they were bound by definite laws to live communally, and those laws are called the law of nations. Hence it is clear that the government we have been discussing here is from natural law and the law of nations.

---

[6] Paulus Orosius, *Historiarum* 1.2 (PL 31.669).
[7] Cicero, *De inventione* 1.2.
[8] *Politics* 1.1.

CHAPTER II

What the priesthood is, and its origin

It is necessary now to take into account that man is not merely ordered to such good as nature can bestow on him, which is to live virtuously, but that he is also ultimately ordered to a supernatural end, which is life eternal. To this is ordered the whole multitude of men living in a society ordered on the principle of virtue. It follows that there must be some one person who will have the direction of all to this end. If it were possible to achieve this end simply through human nature, the directive function would be the king's. For a king by definition is one who has the supreme charge in human affairs. Man however cannot secure eternal life through purely human virtue. As the Apostle says, it is through divine virtue: 'The grace of God, life everlasting.'[1] Thus leadership to that end belongs to a divine not a human king.

Rulership of this sort then belongs to him who is not only man but is also God, that is Jesus Christ, who in making men sons of God has brought them towards eternal life. For thus is he called king, as in the words of Jeremias: 'A king shall reign, and shall be wise'.[2] This office has been confided in him by God the father and shall not be destroyed.[3] And because it is part of the task of a king to clear obstacles from the path to the

---

[1] Rom. 6.23.
[2] Jer. 23.5.
[3] Cf. Dan. 7.14.

desired end and to bestow the remedies and necessary helps for its achievement, therefore Christ, as priest, offered himself as a sacrifice on the cross to God the father and by his death removed the universal obstacle, the injury done to God the father by the common sin of mankind. For this he is that true priest, 'ordained for men',[4] of whom St Paul speaks in book five of his Epistle to the Hebrews. Universal cause must be linked to particular effects. Hence it was necessary to establish certain remedies through which this general benefit might be applied to us in some way.

These remedies are the sacraments of the Church. In them the spiritual merit of the passion of Christ is contained as the virtue of the agent in the instrument which he uses. And hence it was suitable that these sacraments should be of the sense-order, and thus meet the demands of the nature of man, since it is by things of sense that man is led to an understanding of spiritual and intellectual things, according to St Paul's words: 'For the invisible things of him ... understood by the things that are made'.[5] Further, the sacraments are of the sense-order so that as instruments embodying spiritual power, they might be on the same plane as their principal agent, the incarnate Word, to whom they owe their spiritual power.

Since Christ intended to withdraw his physical presence from his Church it was necessary for him to institute ministers who would administer these sacraments to men. These ministers are called *sacerdotes*, sacred ones, because they confer sacred things, because they are leaders in the

[4] Heb. 5.1.
[5] Rom. 1.20.

sacred order, because they teach sacred truths. In all this
they are intermediaries between God and man.

It was necessary then that these ministers should not be
angels but men, men having a spiritual power, as the
Apostle says: 'For every high priest taken from among
men is ordained for men, etc.'[6] This was to be appropriate
both with the instrument they employ (the sacraments)
wherein is a spiritual power under an element of the sense-
order, and also with the principal cause of the salvation
of men, namely the incarnate Word, who inasmuch as he
is both God and man, effects our salvation by his own
power and authority.

From what has been said this definition can be formulated: the priesthood is the spiritual power, given by
Christ to the ministers of his church, of administering the
sacraments to the faithful.

---

[6] Heb. 5.1.

CHAPTER III

The hierarchy of ministers under one supreme head. It is not so necessary for all secular rulers to be hierarchically ordered as it is for ecclesiastical ministers

Power has been given to the Church 'unto edification' as the Apostle says,[1] and must therefore remain in the Church just so long as the Church continues to need building up. This means then that power has been given to the Church until the end of time. Therefore the power was so given to Christ's disciples that it could be passed on by them to others. It needs be that among these ministers some will be superior and complete in their powers and will confer this priesthood on others in ordination and consecration. These are bishops who though not in any way superior to ordinary priests as far as consecrating the true body of Christ is concerned are, in their supervisory role, superior in what touches the faithful. For bishops are important and complete in their power because they can make other priests which lower clergy cannot do. Whatever concerning the faithful people is of a difficult nature is reserved for the bishop's decision and it is by their authority that priests carry out the charge committed to them. In performance of their function priests make use of objects consecrated by bishops — chalice, altar, palls —

[1] 2 Cor. 13.10.

as Dionysius says in his *Concerning the Ecclesiastical Hierarchy* in the chapter 'On Sacerdotal Perfections'.[2]

It is obvious that despite the fact that peoples are divided into different dioceses and communities where bishops rule in spiritual matters, there is yet one church of all the faithful forming one Christian people. Just as in each diocese there is one bishop who is the head of the church of the people there, so in the whole church and Christian people as a whole, there is one supreme head, the Roman pope, successor of Peter. For the church militant is fashioned on the model of the church triumphant which has one head presiding over the whole universe. Hence the Apocalypse: 'And they shall be his people and God himself with them shall be their God';[3] and Osea: 'And the children of Juda shall be gathered together: and they shall appoint themselves one head and shall come up out of the land'.[4] Hence also John: 'They shall be one fold and one shepherd';[5] this text cannot be interpreted as referring only to Christ; it speaks of some one minister ruling everyone in his place. For with the removal of Christ's physical presence it happens on occasion that there are difficulties about the faith, and then diversity of opinion would divide the Church, whose unity demands unity of belief, unless there were some simple authoritative decision through which the unity of the church might be preserved. The one who holds this pre-eminence is Peter and his successor. He does not hold his position because of some decree of a council. He holds it from the very mouth of the Lord

---

[2] Ps.-Dionysius, *De ecclesiastica hierarchia* c.5 PG 3.506.
[3] Apoc. 21.3.
[4] Os. 1.11.
[5] Jo. 10.16.

himself who, before his ascension, being unwilling to leave his church in any way lacking in anything essential to it, gave this charge to Peter alone: 'Feed my sheep':[6] and before his passion he had said already: 'Thou being once converted confirm thy brethren'.[7]

This ordering of all to one supreme head is to be found rather in the ministers of the church than in secular rulers; ecclesiastical ministers have been given their special role of divine worship by the Lord as to men who from his own particular people. Therefore it is by God's decision that there is a subordination of church ministers to one head. But it does not follow that the ordinary faithful are commanded by divine law to be subject in temporalities to any single supreme monarch. Rather do they learn from natural instinct, which comes from God, that they should live as citizens in society and that in order to live well together they should as a result choose the sort of rulers appropriate for the sort of community in question. Neither man's natural tendencies nor divine law commands a single supreme temporal monarchy for everyone. Nor is such as suitable in the lay order as it is in the ecclesiastical. The reasons for this are as follows:

In the first place, because there is diversity among men as to bodies but not as to souls. For as far as souls are concerned, men are in essence alike, for it is the soul which constitutes humanity as a species. So therefore secular power is more diverse, because of the diversity of climates and of the diversity of different physical constitutions, than the spiritual power for which such diversities are less significant. Thus it is not necessary that there should be as

[6] John 21.17.
[7] Luke 22.32.

great a diversity within the one order as within the other.

Secondly, because one man alone cannot rule the world in temporal affairs as can one alone in spiritual affairs. Spiritual power can easily extend its sanction to everyone, near and far, since it is verbal. Secular power, however, cannot so easily extend its sword very far, since it is wielded by hand. It is far easier to extend verbal than physical authority.

Thirdly, because the temporalities of laymen are not communal, as will be shown later; each is master of his own property as acquired through his own industry. There is no need therefore for one to administer temporalities in common since each is his own administrator to do with his own what he wishes. On the other hand, ecclesiastical property was given to the community as a whole; therefore there ought to be someone to preside over the community to act as holder and disposer of all goods on its behalf. It is not then so necessary that one man should rule the whole world in respect of the temporalities of the laity as it is in the case of those of the clergy.

Fourthly, because all the faithful are united in the one universal faith, without which there is no salvation. From time to time questions concerning the faith arise in the different regions and kingdoms and therefore, to avoid breaking the unity of faith through controversy, it is necessary, as has been said already, that there should be one superior in spiritual matters whose decision will put an end to argument. But it does not follow from this that all the faithful should be united in one political community. Rather there are different ways of life and constitutions adapted to the different climates, languages and conditions of peoples, and what is virtuous in one people is not virtuous in another, as is true also for individuals, of whom the Philosopher speaks in *Ethics* Book II,[8] that one thing may be too little for one man and too much for another. For example what would be too much for a school teacher to eat, say ten minas or ounces, would be too little for Milo of Crotona who used to kill a bull in combat with a single blow, as the Commentator says.[9]

We may conclude therefore that the temporal rulership of the world does not demand the rule of a single man as does spiritual rulership, nor can such be deduced from either natural or divine law. Hence the Philosopher shows in the *Politics*[10] that individual states are natural but not that of an empire or one-man rule. Augustine says in Book four of his *City of God* that a society is better and more peacefully ruled when the authority of each realm was confined within its own frontiers. He says also that the cause of the expansion of the Roman empire was its ambition to dominate and the injurious provocation of others.[11] It cannot therefore be deduced from natural law that there should be but one monarch for the temporal order as there is for the spiritual. Nor is what is said in *Decretum* 7 q.1 c.41 a tenable objection, namely its assertion that one should rule and not many. For this text is speaking of what is already one, so that it is inexpedient for it to have many rulers whose spheres of action are not clearly separated, as is illustrated in the case of Remus and Romulus who ruled together without any such clear separation with the result that one killed his brother. The text gives similar examples.

[8] Aristotle, *Nicomachean Ethics* 2.6.
[9] Cf. Aquinas, *Commentum in libros Ethicorum*, 2.6 n. 314.
[10] Aristotle, *Politics* 1.2.
[11] Augustine, *De civitate Dei* 4.3, 4, 15 (*Corpus Scriptorum Ecclesiae Latinae* [= CSEL] 40 sect. 5 pt. 1. 165 ff).

CHAPTER IV

The precedence in time of kingship or priesthood

We must now decide which came first chronologically, kingship or priesthood. It should be known that if the word 'kingdom' is understood in its proper sense it means the government not merely of the household or of the village but of the whole community where is to be found the greatest sufficiency in all the necessities of life. Similarly if the word 'priesthood' is accurately understood, then it can be said that the kingdom preceded the priesthood in time. For as Augustine recounts in the *City of God*[1] the first of the kingdoms was that of the Assyrians which began before the giving of the Law. In Assyria first Belus reigned for sixty-five years, and after his death his son Ninus who, extending his kingdom through the whole of Asia Major except India, ruled for sixty-six years. He had been king for forty-three years when Abraham was born, which was about 1200 before the founding of the city of Rome. Contemporaneous with this kingdom was that of the Sicyonii in Africa, less important though it was at the beginning. Its first king was Egyachus and his son was Europs.

At the same time there was the king of Salem among the worshippers of the true God, whom the Jews call son of Sem who was son of Noah. He is said to have lived up to the time of Isaac.

---

[1] *De civitate Dei* 16.17 (CSEL 40.5.21.158-9).

In this period, with true kings already in existence for a long time, true priesthood did not yet exist nor did it before the time of Chirst, the mediator between God and man. If there were said to be priests among the pagans, these were not true priests because they could neither offer true sacrifice nor did they offer to the true God but only to their own notion of God, Deuteronomy 32.17: 'They sacrificed to devils and not to God'.

If those of the tribe of Levi under the old law were called priests by the people, they were not so in reality but rather prefigurations of true priests. Their sacrifice and their sacraments were not real but figurative, because they did not cleanse from sin nor open the gates of heaven, though they did indicate what was to come in cleansing certain types of irregularity and in opening the temple built by hand, which was the prefiguration of the opening of the mystical temple, not built by hand, by Jesus Christ. Nor did they promise spiritual benefits other than in the form of the temporal; as the Apostle says in his Epistle to the Hebrews: 'The law has a shadow of the good things to come'.[2]

Before the reception of the Law, there was Melchisedech priest of the most high God whose priesthood, though more complete and distinguished than the Levitical priesthood, was yet only figurative and did not constitute true priesthood. It was more complete because it prefigured that element of Christ's priesthood by which that priesthood excelled Aaron's. Aaron as priest did not prefigure Christ as priest, either with respect to permanence of office, as did Melchisedech, of whose beginning and end Scripture

[2] Heb. 10.1.

says nothing, even as Christ had no beginning or end, or with respect to the many other things which the Apostle has to say about the limitations of the Levitical priesthood and the greater excellence of that of Melchisedech, in his Epistle to the Hebrews.[3] But, like the Levitical priesthood, it was nevertheless only a figuration of true priesthood, not true priesthood itself.

Thus there was no true priesthood before Christ Jesus, mediator between God and men, and he has made us participants and representatives of his priesthood.

Since therefore from the time of Abraham before whose birth there were kings of the Assyrians, Sicyonii, Egyptians and certain others, two thousand years elapsed before the coming of Christ (according to the computation of Methodius:[4] or about that length of time according to others), it is clear that there had been kings in the period before the advent of true priesthood whose function was with the needs of human public life. These were true kings, although it must be added that those among the Jews who were anointed also prefigured Christ.

It is to be kept in mind that if the term 'priesthood' be taken in a wide and loose sense, in the sense that a priest of the Law or any other of the figurative or anticipatory kind was said to be a priest, then priesthood occurred contemporaneously with kingship, for among true believers Melchisedech was at once king of Salem and priest of the most high God and from him, according to Jewish accounts and to that of the Master in his *Histories,*[5]

---

[3] Cf. Heb. 7 *passim.*
[4] Cited from Petrus Comestor, *Historia scholastica* Genesis c.41 PL 198.1091.
[5] Petrus Comestor, *op. cit.* Gen. c.46 (*ed. cit.* 1094).

this priesthood was continued through eldest sons down to the time of Aaron. This Melchisedech, according to the Jews, produced a son Arphexat two years after the Flood and there were from the Flood up to Abraham's seventieth year, when the first promise was made to him (as related in Genesis 12), three hundred and seventy years on the literal reading or four hundred and thirty according to some. In the accounts of others, putting the matter simply, the very first kingdom of all was that of the Assyrians, as has been said, whose first king was Belus. Ninus his son succeeding him in the kingdom on his father's death, made an idol called Bel, from which in turn were named the idols of other provinces such as Beelphegor, Beelzebuth and the like, and instituted priests or soothsayers through whom sacrifices were offered to the idols.

From all this it is sufficiently clear that true kingship came into being contemporaneously with priesthood understood as anticipatory or figurative and that it preceded true priesthood by a long time.

CHAPTER V

The precedence in dignity of kingship or priesthood

The arguments presented in the last chapter make it easy to see which comes first in dignity, kingship or priesthood, for what is later in time is generally higher in dignity, as is the perfect in respect of the imperfect and as is end to means. We say therefore that sacerdotal power is greater than the royal and excels it in dignity, because we always find this: what is concerned with the final end is more complete and more worthy and gives direction to what is concerned with an inferior end. Now kingship is ordained to the end that the community may live according to virtue, as has been said already, and it is further ordered, under the care and direction of Christ, whose ministers and representatives are the priests, to a higher end, namely the enjoyment of God. Hence sacerdotal power is higher in dignity than royal power and this is generally agreed. As *Decretum* D.96 c.10 has it: 'As gold is more precious than lead so is the priestly order higher than the royal power'. The decretal *Solitae*[1] states that spirituals excel temporalities even as the sun excels the moon. Hugh of St Victor says that as the spiritual life is worthier than the temporal and the soul, the body, so the spiritual power surpasses the secular or earthly in dignity and honour.[2] St Bernard writes to Pope Eugenius: 'Which seems to you the greater, the

---

[1] *Decretales* 1.33.6.
[2] *De sacramentis* 2.2.4 PL 176.418.

dignity or the power of forgiving sins, or of dividing estates? But there is no comparison';[3] as if to say, the spiritual power is greater so therefore it surpasses the other power in dignity.

Yet though it be said that in principle the priestly is a more dignified function than the royal, it does not follow that it is superior in every respect. For the lesser power, the secular, does not stand related to the greater, the spiritual, as to its origin and derivation in the way that, for example, the power of a pro-consul is related to the emperor who is his superior in all ways since his power derives from the imperial power. The relationship is much more comparable to that between a head of household and a military commander, for the power of neither of these derives from the other but rather both from some superior power. So therefore in temporal matters the temporal power is greater than the spiritual, and in these matters is in no way subject to the spiritual since it is not derived from it. Both take their origin immediately from one supreme power, namely God. Hence the inferior is not subject to the superior in all things but only in those matters in which the supreme power has subordinated the inferior to the superior. What man would argue that because a teacher of letters or moral tutor guides a household to a nobler end, knowledge of truth, than its doctor whose concern is with the lesser end of physical health, the physician should be subject to the teacher in the preparation of his medicines? This sort of subjection would assuredly be inappropriate and the head of the household who was responsible for bringing them into his house did not subordinate the one to the other in this way. The priest, then, is greater in spirituals than is the prince and conversely, the prince in temporalities, though it is granted that absolutely speaking the priest is the greater even as the spiritual is greater than the temporal.

The authorities cited earlier prove this. For though gold is certainly more precious than lead, yet lead is not made from gold, and this is expressly stated in *Decretum* 2 q.7 c.41. It must be understood, however, that what has been said refers only to the true priesthood of Christ. For pagan priesthood and its cult of the gods was for the sake of temporal goods ordered to the common good of the people, which charge was the king's. Hence pagan priests were subject to kings and kingship was greater than the priesthood, since the power of him who has charge of the common good is greater than and superior to the power of one who has the charge of what is only a particular good. Similarly in the Old Law, all that the priesthood promised directly was temporal goods, although these were to be set before the people as coming from the true God, not from devils. Thus even in the Old Law the priesthood was less worthy than royal power and was subject to it because the priest was not concerned to direct the king to any end higher than the common good of the community which was his charge. The opposite is true in the New Law.

It is worth remembering that God in his wonderful providence disposed that in Rome, his chosen chief seat for the Christian priesthood, the custom gradually took root that the rulers of the city should of their own will be more subject to priests than in other cities. This they did not from any duty of justice since they were in principle superior to priests, but as a symbol of the greater excellence of the priesthood of the future. As Valerius said: 'We in this city have always put religion before all other things, even in those where the glory of high majesty wished to attract notice, wherefore the authorities did not hesitate to serve sacred things, judging that they would obtain sway over men if they regularly and correctly placated the divine power.'[4] Likewise because in the future it was to be in France that the religion of the Christian priesthood was to flourish best, divine providence ensured that among the Gauls the pagan priests called druids gave definition to Gallic life, as Julius Caesar wrote in his *On the Gallic War*.[5] Thus is the priesthood of Christ of higher rank than royal power.

---

[4] Valerius Maximus, *Factorum dictorumque memorabilium* 1.1, 9.
[5] *De bello gallico* 6.13.

CHAPTER VI

The priesthood is not first in the order of causality. The way in which the pope has lordship of ecclesiastical property

There are some who wish to elevate the pre-eminence of the priesthood over the royal dignity to the degree where the priesthood is not merely superior in dignity, as discus· sed earlier, but even superior in the order of causality. They claim that the secular power is contained within the spiritual power and is established by it. It now remains, therefore, to discuss in what way the pope who has the chief place among Christ's priests has or has not got secular power. The method of argument will be to examine firstly, papal lordship of property and then, secondly, it being established that he is not the true lord but the administrator in both principle and practice, whether he has at least the original and primary authority, as superior and as one who exercises jurisdiction.

On the first point what has to be examined to start with, is the form of power he has over the property of ecclesiastics in so far as they are ecclesiastics. Here it must be appreciated that ecclesiastical property, as ecclesiastical property, has been given to communities, not to individual persons. So therefore, no one person has proprietary right and lordship over ecclesiastical property. It is the community concerned which itself has these, as in the case, for example, of the church of Chartres or some similar church, where it is the community which has right of lordship over its property. An individual person may have a right of usage for his maintenance judged according to his needs and considering what is appropriate for his rank. He has this not as an individual in his own right but purely as part and member of the community. Difference of rank is relevant here for there is a difference between an ordinary canon, who has no right other than the one just mentioned, and the member who is the principal and head of the community, the bishop. The congregation would not be an ordered unity unless it had one head and chief member, and he has not only the right of use of the goods of the community according to the needs of his position in the manner already mentioned, but has, in addition, general administration and dispensation of all the property of the community, allocating here to someone his just due, dispensing there in good faith as seems to him expedient for the good of the whole. This is the position of any bishop in any cathedral church.

It is not only the particular community of ecclesiastics which is joined in unity of the spirit. There is a certain general unity among all ecclesiastical communities since all together make up the one church united with one principal member, the lord pope, on whom falls the charge of the Church as a whole. He therefore as head and supreme member of the universal church is general steward of all ecclesiastical goods whether spiritual or temporal. He is not indeed lord of them, for only the community of the universal Church is mistress and proprietress of all goods generally and individual communities and churches have lordship in the property allocated to them. In like manner also, individual persons, whoever they may be, do not enjoy lordship; principal members have stewardship only, except in so far as they draw recompense for their service, according to the need of person and position,

with perhaps something in addition granted by the general
steward, with good faith the determining factor, according
to the division of ecclesiastical property into four categories, as papal law provides, *Decretum* 12 q.2.[1]

From all this, it appears that they speak ill who say
that no individual other than the pope, nor any corporate
body or community has right and lordship in ecclesiastical
property. They say that the pope is not only general
administrator and steward but that he alone is true lord
and proprietor of ecclesiastical property. They argue that
he can make decisions about it and alienate it as he
wishes and that what he decides has legal validity,
though it is granted that he commits sin if he acts without
reasonable cause. They urge further that other prelates or
even princes or communities do not hold true lordship but
are only the guardians, protectors and stewards of such
properties. This is false as has been shown, for the pope is
no more universal lord of all ecclesiastical property than are
lesser prelates lords of the property of their chapters. The
pope is in fact manager and steward of ecclesiastical
property; further, he takes for himself a greater share of
the common store according to the demands of his position,
which is that of the holder of fulness of power, than other
prelates who are called only to a part of the pastoral charge.

Hence Augustine in his letter to Boniface speaking of
prelates and including all of them says: 'If we possess a
sufficiency for private use, these things are not ours: we
hold the stewardship of them. Let us not therefore
guiltily usurp ownership for ourselves'.[2] And the Apostle

---

[1] C.27-30.
[2] Ep. 185 c.9 35 PL 33.809.

says, and here he is not excluding Peter and the pope: 'Let a man so account of us as of the ministers of Christ and the dispensers of the mysteries of God'.[3] Bernard also spoke about temporal possessions to Pope Eugenius, Book II: 'Suppose you claim them for yourself on the basis of some reason or other, it cannot be by apostolic right, for the Apostle could not give you what he himself did not possess. "Silver and gold", he says, "I have none".[4] What he had, he gave, namely care of all the Churches, not indeed lordship. Listen to what he says:[5] "Neither as lording it over the clergy, but being examples to the flock'".[6] That is Bernard's view of the matter.

From all this, it is evident that clergy as clergy, and monks as monks, are not precluded from having lordship of property, at least in common, for their vow does not incapacitate them from holding or owing personal and common property, as it does in the case of some religious. Since the founders of churches intended to transfer lordship and proprietary right of the properties they were giving principally and directly to the community of the individual church, for the use of those who were serving God, and not to the pope, it is obvious that it is the community itself which has immediate and true lordship of its property and not the pope or any lesser prelate. Otherwise the way of life of these clergy would not be any different as far as property was concerned from that of the friars minor, whose vow renders them incapable of property lordship either individually or collectively. For they have only

[3] 1 Cor. 4.1.
[4] Acts 3.6.
[5] 1 Peter 5.3.
[6] *De consid.* 2.6.

the usage of fact, as Pope Nicholas says.[7] In order that the legal position of the property given to them should not be vague and obscure — it is ecclesiastical property that is in question because it has been given to churchmen — the pope takes on himself and the church the right of lordship of such property. The belief is quite unacceptable that the position in property matters of the secular clergy and other religious is exactly the same as this. Pope Nicholas himself says in the same decretal that a monk and a servant, the one for his monastery, the other for his lord, can acquire right and lordship in anything. The pope then is not sole lord but the general steward, the bishop or abbot the particular or immediate steward, while true proprietary right rests with the community.

Further, it cannot be argued that the pope has right and lordship of such property not in his private capacity but in his public office, in that he acts as general vicar of Jesus Christ, who is principal lord of all property. Such a proposition carries no force because it is as God that Christ is lord of all property, ecclesiastical and non-ecclesiastical. As man, he does not have communication or contact with those who are in the church; those who have given property to the church did not intend to transfer proprietary right and lordship to Christ either as God, because everything already is his, or as man, because he now has no use for such authority. What they intended was to transfer proprietary right to Christ's ministers. Hence such property belongs to the Church as proprietor, to the prelates as stewards, as has been said.

It follows from this that the pope has no authority to take away ecclesiastical property at will, claiming that

[7] VIo 5.12.3 (Nicholas IV).

whatever he commands has legal validity. This would be true were he lord of all ecclesiastical property; since, however, he is but steward for the community, he must keep good faith with it and he has no power therefore over this property, except such as the common necessity and welfare of the church requires. Thus it is written in 2 Cor. 13 and 10 that God has given power to prelates for building up, not for destruction.[8] Hence if the pope deprives anyone arbitrarily, not in good faith, what he does is illegal. This means that not only is he obliged to do penance for his sin as if guilty of misusing his own property, but also, as betrayer of a trust, he is bound to make restitution either from his patrimony should he have one or from what he has acquired, since he has cheated in what is not his.

A monastic community can act to depose its abbot and a church might do the same to its bishop, if it has been established that he has squandered the property of the monastery or church and that he has broken faith in taking for his private gain what was for the common good. In the same way, should a pope betray his trust in taking the property of churches for reasons other than the common good, which as chief bishop is his especial charge, he can be deposed should he not, on admonition, make amends. This argument is based on *Decretum* D.40 *c. Si papa*[9] where it is said: 'those who can judge all cannot be judged by anyone, except if detected in error of faith' on which the Gloss comments: 'Should he be detected in any other fault and having been admonished does not amend and is giving scandal to the church, the same shall be done', though others say, arguing from *Decretum* D.21 *c. Nunc*

[8] 2 Cor. 10.8, 13.10.
[9] D.40 c.6.

autem[10] that this should only be done by a general council.

If the pope knows that there are persons, whether ecclesiastics or laymen, who are laying complaint against him on the score of unjust stewardship as they are permitted and indeed under obligation to do, he can in no mannner legally remove them or depose them from what is theirs; he has no authority from God to do this. They set their mouths against heaven[11] and do injury to our most holy father the pope who preach that his will is absolute in this way when it ought rather to be supposed that his will is not contrary to law and that he would not wish to deprive anyone of what is his without reasonable cause since to do so is illegal. God does not wish anyone to be deprived of what has been given to him, if he has incurred no fault, for as the Apostle says in his Epistle to the Romans: 'The gifts of God are without repentance';[12] on account of men's sins, he says 'It repenteth me that I have made man';[13] because of the sins of the Egyptians, he made the plunder of the Hebrews. He wanted the just man to take nothing and nothing to be taken from him, as in Job 36: 'He giveth judgment to the poor. He will not take his eyes from the just and he placeth kings on the throne for ever'.[14] So therefore, since it is the trust of stewardship which God has given to Peter and the pope, the pope may not go against the express will of God to take away arbitrarily from anyone any right of administration which has been received justly and properly, if he has not manifestly been at fault. This then is the power that the pope has over ecclesiastical property.

[10] D.21 c.7.
[11] Cf. Psalms 72.9.
[12] Rom. 11.29.
[13] Gen. 6.7.
[14] Job 36.6-7.

CHAPTER VII

The power of the pope over lay property

What has been said already makes clear what the true relationship of the pope to lay property is. He is even less the lord of it, nor is he its steward, unless perhaps in some extreme need of the Church. In such a case of necessity he would be acting as one who declares what the law is, not as steward. In order to prove this principle, it must be remembered that lay property is not granted to the community as a whole as is ecclesiastical property, but is acquired by individual people through their own skill, labour and diligence, and individuals, as individuals, have right and power over it and valid lordship; each person may order his own and dispose, administer, hold or alienate it as he wishes, so long as he causes no injury to anyone else, since he is lord. Such properties therefore are not mutually interordered or interconnected nor do they have any common head who might dispose of and administer them, since each person may arrange for his own what he will. Thus neither prince nor pope has lordship or administration of such properties. For the reason that sometimes the peace of everybody is disturbed because of these possessions, when someone takes what belongs to another and also because at times some men, through excessive love of their own, do not place it at the service of the common need and welfare of the country, a ruler has been established by the people to take charge of such situations, a judge between the just and the unjust, a punisher of injustices, a measurer of the just proportion owed by each to the common need and welfare. The pope is in a similar position by virtue of that supreme headship which he holds not merely over the clergy but generally over all believers, in so far as they are the faithful. In any major necessity of faith and morals all the possessions of the faithful are common property and must be shared, even the chalices of churches. The pope, as general teacher of faith and morals, has the power to manage the goods of the faithful and to decide what should be expended on the common defence of the faith, which might otherwise be destroyed by pagan invasion or some such disaster, and so great and obvious might this need be that he could demand tithes and fixed contributions from individual members of the faithful, though these should be according to their means, since some people for no reasonable cause might otherwise be burdened more than others in giving aid for defence of the faith, a matter which concerns everybody. Such a disposition by the pope is no more than a declaration of law. He would have the power to coerce by ecclesiastical censure those who disobeyed or spoke against his measures. With the same sanction the pope could compel the faithful to contribute to the full extent of the need in the case of parishes where a parish priest because of increased numbers has been forced to take on the services of a number of assistant priests while the revenue of the parish has remained at its old level. This also is a case where the pope's action is a declaration of law. The pope has no power to make rulings concerning the property of laymen beyond this type of case involving the common spiritual good. Each individual person may dispose of his own as he wishes, except in time of necessity, when the prince may dispose of them in the interest of the common temporal good. In cases not of necessity but of some spiritual utility or where it is agreed that lay property has nothing to contribute for such utility or necessity, the pope may not compel anyone, but he may grant indulgences to the faithful for giving help and, in my view, no power beyond this has been given him.

CHAPTER VIII

The pope does not hold from Christ any jurisdiction over the property of laymen, because Christ himself had no such jurisdiction

To have proprietary and lordship right over property is not the same thing as having jurisdiction over it, which is the right of deciding what is just or unjust in matters pertaining thereto. A prince has the power of judging matters though he does not himself enjoy possession of the property in question. It is now necessary to find out whether Christ has given the pope any such power or jurisdiction, as some people argue. To prove this proposition wrong, it will be proved that Christ himself as man did not have it. Then it will be established that even if Christ as man did have such jurisdiction and power, he did not pass it on to Peter.

It must be understood that Christ was a king in a three-fold sense. The first sense is the same as that in which God the father is king, namely not merely of all men, but of all creation, for all creatures are subject to him, as is written in Ecclesiasticus: 'There is one most high creator, almighty, and a powerful king.'[1] This authority has not been given to any man; it was not given to Peter to be a creator.

Secondly, Christ can be considered as God made man. In this capacity, he is said to be king of men because what

[1] Eccli. 1.8.

he did in the flesh leads us to membership of a kingdom, not indeed of this world, but of a higher one, the kingdom of heaven. Hence not only is he called priest, but also king, as Jeremias: 'And a king shall reign and be wise'.[2] Hence the royal priesthood derives from him, that of which St Peter has spoken; 'But you are a chosen generation, a royal priesthood'.[3] But further than this: the Gloss adds that all the faithful, in so far as they are his members, one with Christ the head through faith and charity, are kings and priests. The Apocalypse says: 'Thou hast made us to our God a kingdom and priests in thy blood',[4] that is, through the faith of thy passion. All the same, the ministers of the church participate more fully in this royal priesthood, for what they offer to God is not only what all just men offer him, namely the offering of a contrite and humble heart, but in addition they offer public sacrifice in which divine virtue is contained in a spiritual way both for themselves and for the people as a whole, as was said earlier.[5] They lead the rest to a share in the heavenly kingdom not only through the force of their love but also by virtue of their function of teaching and of administering the sacraments.

If it is argued that Christ as man was king — and here I mean king of a temporal kingdom, having direct and immediate authority in temporalities — this is altogether false. For he shared our poverty as with all our unblameworthy deficiencies, as St John Damascene teaches us.[6]

[2] Jer. 23.5.
[3] 1 Pet. 2.9.
[4] Apoc. 5.9, 10.
[5] Cf. c. 2 above.
[6] *De fide orthodoxa* 3.20 PG 94.1082.

St John gives Christ's own words: 'My kingdom is not of this world'.[7] The Gloss here cites St Augustine: 'Hear me, gentiles and Jews; I am not impeding your domination in this world'. St John Chrysostom in the Gloss on the same text comments that he did not have kingship as earthly kings have it but had his rulership from above in a more lofty and perfect form. Pope Leo said in a sermon for the Epiphany: 'The magi reasoned in a purely human way and thought that he should be sought after in the royal city: but he who had taken on the work of a servant being come to serve, not to be served, had chosen Bethlehem for his nativity and Jerusalem for his passion'.[8] Hence Herod misunderstood; hearing that a king had been born he feared that it would be a king who would usurp his own temporal lordship. Chrysostom said on Matthew:[9] 'Herod ignored the prophecy of Micheas which was now fulfilled,[10] "And thou Bethlehem art by no means the least among the princes of Juda, out of thee shall be come forth unto me that is to be the ruler in Israel: and his going forth is from the beginning, from the days of eternity". If he had considered that he whose days are of eternity could not be a temporal king, he would not have fallen into error of such magnitude. For this reason Eusebius said[11] that the Herodites erred in saying that because he was anointed he was therefore to be king of temporalities, for he was not anointed like the kings of earth, with any material oil, but with a spiritual oil, namely the oil of

7 Jo. 18.36 and Aquinas, *Catena aurea*, for the commentary.
8 *Sermo* 32.2 PL 54.235.
9 Matth. 2.6 PG 56.640.
10 Mich. 5.2.
11 *Historia Ecclesiastica* 1.3 PG 20.74.

gladness above his fellows.¹² And therefore he is not king
of this world but of that kingdom of which the Prophet
Daniel spoke: 'His power is an everlasting power and his
kingdom shall not be destroyed'.¹³ St Luke records Christ's
reply to one of the crowd who said to him: '"Master,
speak to my brother that he divide the inheritance with
me". But he said to him, "Man, who hath appointed me
judge or divider over you? Take heed and beware all
covetousness"'.¹⁴

According then to all this evidence of the holy expositors
of scripture it is clear that Christ had no authority or
judicial power over temporalities, but gave example of
virtue. Thus St Bernard explaining the last-cited text to
Eugenius: 'It cannot be shown that any of the apostles
ever sat as judge of men or as an adjudicator of boundaries
or as a distributor of lands. I read that the apostles had
to stand as men under accusation; I do not read that they
sat as accusers. That was for later development; it did not
happen then.'¹⁵ Later he showed what power Christ had on
earth in citing the text: 'So that you may know that the
son of man has power to forgive sins'.¹⁶ Further, St
Jerome explains the text, 'Render to Caesar the things that
are Caesar's'¹⁷ by saying that Jesus paid the tribute for
himself and for Peter, and that he rendered to God the
things that are God's in submitting himself to the will of
the father.¹⁸ St Hilary said about the same text: 'Christ

---

¹² Cf. Ps. 44.8.
¹³ Dan. 7.14.
¹⁴ Luke 12.13-15.
¹⁵ *De consideratione* 1.6 PL 182.735.
¹⁶ *Ibid*. col. 736. The text is Matth. 9.6.
¹⁷ Matth. 22.21.
¹⁸ *In Matth*. 22 PL 26.169.

ordered us to give our riches to Caesar, but to preserve for God the innocence of our conscience'.[19] If it is argued that he was not bound to pay the tribute but paid it to avoid scandal, as was said about the temple tax,[20] the objection is not valid. For it was not to Caesar that the didrachma was paid; it was a temple due, owed by all the first-born of Israel in remembrance of the death of the first-born in Egypt. The Jews thought that Jesus was the first-born of Joseph and saw that Peter was first among the disciples of Christ and so held each of them liable for payment. But Christ was not liable for he was not the son of Joseph. Nor was Peter, for his place as principal disciple did not make him a first-born son. Thus when Jesus paid it was only because he wished to avoid scandal. The position about the tribute to Caesar was quite different; Christ ordered that to be paid always. Pope Urban cites this text about finding the didrachma in the fish's mouth to prove that all clergy and churches are liable to pay tribute to the emperor on their secular possessions.[21] From all the foregoing, it appears that Christ as man had no dominion over temporalities and that no priest at all may claim to be Christ's vicar in this, for Christ has not granted to anyone what he did not have himself. As he said himself: 'Amen, amen I say to you: the servant is not greater than his lord: neither is the apostle greater than he that sent him'.[22] And again, 'The disciple is not above the master, nor the servant above his lord'.[23]

---

[19] *In Matth*. 22 PL 9.1045.
[20] Cf. Matth. 17.23-26.
[21] *Decretum* 23 q.8 c.22.
[22] Jo. 13.16.
[23] Matth. 10.24.

CHAPTER IX

*Arguments that Christ had jurisdiction over
the property of laymen, and replies to them*

There are perhaps some who assert the opposite, deducing from Matthew 21, where it is related how Christ
took a whip to drive out those who were buying and
selling in the temple, that he would not have performed
this action if he had not held authority over lay property.
Hence it is said in 1. q. 3 c. *Ex multis*[1] that while pronouncing the authority of his command he said: 'Do not
make my Father's house into a house of commerce'. Again,
it can be read in Matthew[2] how he sent his disciples to
fetch an ass and a colt, with the explanation that the Lord
had need of them. Also, he sent demons into pigs which
promptly hurled themselves into the sea, without having
made any previous enquiry as to who owned them.[3]
Again, it is related in St Matthew's last chapter how after
the Resurrection, he said: 'All authority in heaven and on
earth has been given to me' and the Gloss: 'To him who
first was dead and crucified'.[4] Further, they read Ps. 2.
8-9 as addressed by the Father to the Son: 'Ask of me and
I will give thee the Gentiles for thy inheritance etc. and
the utmost parts of the earth. Thou shalt rule them with
a rod of iron etc.'. From these arguments they conclude
that Christ as man had power in temporal affairs.

[1] *Decretum* 1 q.3 c.9.
[2] Matth. 21.2-3.
[3] Matth. 8.30-32.
[4] Matth. 28.18 and Aquinas, *Catena aurea in Matthaeum* 28.

All such arguments can be easily dismissed when one appreciates that something can be attributed to Christ as God which was not in his power as man. But let each argument be considered separately. What was said about the expulsion of the merchants is answered in the Gloss on D. 10 c. *Quoniam idem* where it is stated, 'Christ performed certain actions as emperor and certain others as priest, as is testified in *On consecration* D. 2 c. *Sacerdos*, not because one and the same person exercises both these functions or ought to exercise them, but to show that both powers have their origin in him, as God. For these two, empire and papacy, have the same source, as is stated in the Preface to Nov. 6'.[5] Chrysostom, commenting on this Matthew text said that Christ's expulsion of the merchants was executed by virtue of his divine authority, thereby showing how in the temple of God there ought not to be any ministers but spiritual ones, who bear the image of God, not that of any earthly individual, so that there should be in God's house neither commerce nor lust for profit, lest Jesus should need to enter in anger and severity, having no choice but to use a whip to make a house of prayer out of a den of thieves.[6]

The argument concerning the ass can be dealt with in the same way. Christ here exercised authority as God. Hence the Gloss on the text, 'The Lord has need of them' says 'The Lord speaks absolutely and simply to suggest that he is lord not only of the beasts but also of men; to him all things are subject.'[7]

---

[5] *Glossa ordinaria ad Decretum* D.10 c.8.
[6] *Opus imperfectum in Matth. Homil.* 38 PG 56.841.
[7] *Glossa ordinaria ad Matth.* 21.2.

A similar type of reply can be made to the deduction from the pigs episode, though it is possible that they were wild pigs, without an owner, no one having a use for them since the Jews did not eat pork.

The conclusion drawn from the text, 'All authority in heaven and on earth has been given to me', is answered by Jerome with his explanation that it is all spiritual, not all temporal power, that has been given: 'Power is given to him in heaven and earth so that he who previously ruled in heaven might now rule on earth through the faith of those who believe in him'.[8] How he might reign through this faith is explained in a later argument. Or one can say with Remigius that all power was given in the Incarnation to him who died, precisely because he is God and all-powerful.[9] This omnipotence was indeed known to the angels in heaven, but it was not known on earth until after the resurrection when he sent preachers to announce the word of God and to preach that Christ was the all-powerful God. Thus all authority was given to him in heaven and earth at the Incarnation, not in any sense of receiving it, since he had had it from the beginning, but in the sense of its becoming manifest and taken notice of.

I turn now to the argument based on 'Ask of me ...' The reference is to the kingdom which through faith guides us to heaven. Hence in the text: 'I will give thee the Gentiles for thy inheritance', *Gentiles* is to be understood as meaning those adhering to Christ by faith.[10] Similarly, 'thou shalt rule them with a rod of iron' is explained by

[8] Aquinas, *Catena aurea, loc. cit.*
[9] Aquinas, *ibid.*
[10] Aquinas, *Expositio in Ps. 2.*

the Gloss, 'with unbending justice'[11] which is to say, through faith, for the just man lives by faith;[12] 'And thou shalt break them in pieces like a potter's vessel' is to be read with the Gloss: 'from the filth of carnality and by cleansing from sin'.[13] For thus is the yoke of the law and of sin removed by Christ from his members, as the Gloss has it. The reign of Christ over men through faith should not be understood as if the converted through faith thereby became subject to the vicar of Christ in property matters in the same way as men are subject to their kings. For this would mean that Christ had changed his kingdom into an earthly one, as Herod feared. Rather should it be said that he reigns through faith because what in men is all-important and supreme, the intellect they subject to Christ, bringing it captive into the service of the faith.[14] The opinion of the saints is that it is the hearts of men and not their property which Christ is said to rule through faith.

11 *Glossa interlinearis in Ps. 2.*
12 Cf. Rom. 1.17.
13 *Glossa interlinearis in Ps. 2.*
14 Cf. 2 Cor. 10.5.

CHAPTER X

Granted that Christ had jurisdiction over lay property, still he did not hand it on to Peter

Even supposing that Christ as man had the sort of authority and power we have been talking about, nevertheless he did not hand it on to Peter, and so the argument that it belongs to the pope as Peter's successor does not stand. For the episcopal and temporal powers are distinct not only in themselves, but they are to be distinguished also by the subject in which they are found. The emperor, having no superior over him, is greater in temporal matters, as the pope is in spiritual matters.

An examination of the relationship of Christ and the Church will demonstrate this. Christ is head of the Church as is stated in Ephes. 5; and according to Ambrose[1] it must be understood that his headship is according to his human nature, not only according to his divinity. But what in the head are undifferentiated are in the members sometimes distinguished by subject. For all the senses are in the head but are not so in any particular one of the other members. It is as if axiomatic that things are more differentiated in the originated than in the original, in the effects than in the cause, in the inferior than in the superior. So therefore it does not follow that even if Christ, as man, had both powers he conferred both on Peter. Rather did he give the spiritual alone to Peter, leaving the corporal to Caesar, who received it directly from God.

[1] Ephes. 5.23 and *glossa ordinaria*.

The same is proved from the major premise. Christ as man had a certain power in spiritual matters which he might have conferred on Peter and on the other ministers of the Church, but yet he did not do so. This was the power which theologians call the power of excellence which inhered in Christ's humanity only whereby the effect of a sacrament might be conferred without the sacrament itself or without the spoken word, that sacraments might be conferred in his name, that he could institute new sacraments. This was a power of the spiritual order that he could have conferred on Peter but did not; as the theologians say and as Richard says in his book *On the forgiveness of sins,*[2] Christ could dismiss sins whereas our power is not his, but only to remit them. Hence it is the more to be denied that even if Christ did have power in temporal affairs he necessarily gave it to Peter, especially as this is not found specifically granted to him; express mention is to be found only of the spiritual power granted to him, the power to forgive sins. Hence all the arguments which attribute anything to Peter because Christ even in his humanity had that same power are of no validity, unless it can be proved that the power had been expressly granted.

Again, the general principle is clear from the perfection of the sacrifice of the New Testament. The more a thing has perfect being, the more its being is distinct. Thus we see that sexual distinction is not as complete in plants as in animals. Hence male and female can be together in one and the same plant and yet are not distinguished by subject. In animals, however, male and female are distinguished by

[2] Richard of St Victor, *De potestate ligandi et solvendi* c.24 PL 196.1176.

subject, unless there occurs an error of nature, as happens with hermaphrodites. Under the Old Law, when priesthood was less perfect, the royal and sacerdotal powers were distinct in themselves and by the subject in which they were found. Therefore, so much the more did God wish them to be distinct by subject in the New Testament.

The same conclusion can be drawn from a comparison of the Church, instituted by God, to works of art. A home would seem to be imperfect, deficient in equipment, not self-sufficient if one person is occupied in many tasks. The Philosopher says on this point in Book 6 of his *Politics*[3] that the poor, not having a supply of servants nor that abundance of possessions needed to complete a household, use daughters and wives as servants. But the Church of Christ is likened to a house, as in 'O Israel how great is the house of God'[4] and in Matthew, 'My house shall be called the house of prayer'.[5] Therefore since God has provided it with sufficient means, it is inappropriate that one person alone should be entrusted with such diverse duties as the priestly function and royal lordship, in which indeed kings minister to God, as Romans 13: 'For he beareth not the sword in vain. For he is God's minister'.[6] Perish the thought that what in art and nature is unbecoming, should find a place in what has been instituted by God. The Philosopher says in Book 1 of the *Politics*[7] that nature has nothing comparable to show to the smiths who make Delphic swords. For amongst the Delphinians a multipur-

---

[3] Aristotle, *Politics* 6.8.
[4] Baruch 3.24.
[5] Matth. 21.13.
[6] Rom. 13.4.
[7] Aristotle, *Politics* 1.1.

pose sword used to be made for the use of the poor. Nature does nothing similar; much less, then, the author of nature. The Philosopher also observes that every instrument is best made when intended for one and not for many uses.

The same conclusion emerges if what is contentious or injurious is considered. For two reasons, God wanted there to be two powers not only distinct in themselves but also by the subject in which they are found, that they should not be held by one and the same person as the primary authority. Firstly, so long as the prince needs the priest for spiritual affairs and the priest the prince for temporal affairs, that love and charity without which members of the Church cannot live will be promoted through the need of these members one for another and their mutual support. This could not happen if one person held both powers. The Apostle suggests this in Romans 12 when he says: 'We are one in Christ, everyone members of another, having different gifts'[8] and again, 'If the whole body were the eye, where would be the hand and if the whole were the hand, where would be the eye?'[9] The other reason is lest the charge of temporal authority should make the priest or the pope less solicitous for the direction of the spiritual. The Apostle refers to this when instructing Timothy: 'No man being a soldier to God entangleth himself with secular businesses etc.'[10]

For these two reasons then, God the all-wise disposer wished the two powers to be distinct not only in themselves but also by the subject in which they are found.

[8] Rom. 12.6.
[9] 1 Cor. 12.17.
[10] 2 Tim. 2.4.

Cyprian makes reference to both reasons in D. 10 c. *Quoniam idem,*[11] and Pope Nicholas exactly similarly, D.96 c. *Cum ad uerum.*[12] Likewise the Saviour says in Matthew 20: 'The princes of the Gentiles lord it over them, it shall not be so among you'.[13] Further, all the Apostles received the same power as Peter, as may be seen in Matthew 18[14] and D.21 c. *In nouo,*[15] where it is said that Peter was the first to receive the power of binding and loosing; the rest of the Apostles received honour and power in equal fellowship *with* him. It is not said *from* him. In this conferring, Christ did not withold from the others anything he had given to Peter, though it is apparent from the way he spoke that he wanted Peter to be superior, as head of the Church for the sake of preserving its unity. The present position must be understood exactly as it was among the Apostles, namely that just as then, whatever one like Peter could do so could another, so now in common law whatever the pope can do so can any other bishop, the difference being that the pope's power is a universal one, whilst that of the other bishops is restricted to their own dioceses. No one claims, however, that the remainder of the bishops, in so far as they are vicars of Christ and successors of the other Apostles, have authority and lordship of temporal property and that appeal lies from a secular ruler in a temporal case to the local bishop or to the local parish priest, who some say has the same power in his parish as has the bishop in his diocese. It follows

---

[11] *Decretum* D.10 c.8.
[12] *Decretum* D.96 c.6.
[13] Matth. 20.25.
[14] Matth. 18.8.
[15] *Decretum* D.21 c.2.

then that no one should claim that the pope has such powers on the universal scale.

Again, when the disciples were asking who would be the greater in the kingdom of Christ to come (they were thinking his kingdom would be a kingdom of this world), the Lord replied: 'The kings of the Gentiles lord it over them; and they that have power over them are called beneficent. But you not so.[16] Bernard, expounding this text in Book 2 of his *To Pope Eugenius* says: 'It is quite clear that the apostles are forbidden to exercise lordship. Dare you venture then on usurpation: either acting the lord over an apostolate or the apostle over a lordship. Obviously you are forbidden both. You must not think yourself excepted from the number of those of whom God complained: "They have reigned but not by me: they have been princes and I knew not."[17] And later: 'This is the apostolic model: lordship is forbidden, service is commanded.' And again: 'Go out, I say, Eugenius, into the world. For the field is the world and it is given into your charge. Go into it not as a lord but as a steward.'[18] It is not then from Christ or his vicar Peter that the pope has lordship. Bernard again, in Book 1: 'Your jurisdiction is over sins not possessions, since it is because of the former not the latter that you have accepted the keys of the kingdom of heaven.' And later: 'These things have kings and princes as their judges. Why do you trespass on alien territory? Not because you are unworthy, but because it is an unworthy thing for you to concern yourselves with such

[16] Luke 22.25-26.
[17] Osea 8.4.
[18] *De consideratione* 2.6.

matters, when you ought rather to be concerned with greater matters.'[19]

Taking the argument further: popes have pronounced that spiritual and temporal powers are distinct, not dependent one on the other, as in D.10 c. *Quoniam idem,*[20] D.96 c. *Cum ad uerum,*[21] c. *Duo sunt.*[22] They are distinct to the extent that one power is not reduced to dependence on the other, but just as the spiritual power derives immediately from God, so does the temporal. Hence the imperial authority is from God only, as is found stated in 23 q.4 c. *Quesitum.*[23] Because the pope does not have his sword from the emperor, neither is the converse true, as is shown in D.63 c. *Si imperator.*[24] For it is the army which makes the emperor, as D.93 c. *Legimus* states.[25] Pope Alexander ruled that no appeal lies to the pope from a secular ruler in a secular case and also that temporalities were not of his jurisdiction: see his decretals, *Extra. De appellationibus.* c. *Si duobus*[26] and *Qui filii sint legitimi* c. *Causam.*[27] There is a case of an appeal from a bishop to a secular prince in *Extra. De foro competenti* c. *Verum;*[28] but here the bishop is acting as a secular judge: see also, *Extra. De iudiciis* c. *Ceterum*[29] and the Preface to *Nov.*6. The Church pays tribute to the emperor, 11 q.1 c.

---

[19] *De consideratione* 1.6.
[20] *Decretum* D.10 c.8.
[21] *Ibid.* D.96 c.6.
[22] *Ibid.* D.96 c.10.
[23] *Ibid.* 23 q.4 c.45.
[24] *Ibid.* D.96 c.11.
[25] *Ibid.* D.93 c.24.
[26] *Decretales* 2.28.7.
[27] *Ibid.* 4.17.7.
[28] *Ibid.* 2.2.7.
[29] *Ibid.* 2.2.5.

Magnum,[30] where Ambrose cites the example of Christ who did pay tribute, as also the Apostle's text: 'Let every soul be subject to the higher powers etc.'[31] and 1 Peter 2: 'Be ye subject therefore to your lords, whether it be to the king etc.'.[32] The same position is established in the same *quaestio, c. Si tributum.*[33]

Many arguments of a similar nature can be brought forward to show that the pope has neither the power of both swords nor any jurisdiction in temporal affairs unless it has been granted to him out of piety by a secular ruler. Commentators on canon law whose opinion carries weight in the Church say this, even in a case where the argument might have seemed weaker. Thus Hostiensis, commenting on *Extra. De iudiciis* c. *Vergentis,*[34] where the pope has ordered the property of heretics to be confiscated, asks: 'What business of the pope's are temporal possessions?' and replies, following his master Innocent IV, that truly they were no concern of his, but he acted with the permission of the emperor who was then at Padua. It seems remarkable that the emperor Constantine is said to have given the kingdom of Italy to the Church with full temporal jurisdiction and that the Church received it as a gift if it already held it by right. On this line of argument, it would not have been a donation granted to blessed Sylvester but a return of what he already had. Yet the Church holds a contrary view, as in D.96 c. *Constantinus.*[35]

---

[30] *Decretum* 11 q.1 c.28.
[31] Rom. 13.1.
[32] 1 Pet. 2.13.
[33] *Decretum* 11 q.1 c.27.
[34] Hostiensis, *Apparatus* 5.7.9.
[35] *Decretum* D.96 c.14.

Some people think they can escape from some of the foregoing arguments by making a pithy distinction. They argue that secular power belongs to the pope immediately and as the prime source of authority, that he does not have immediate executive power but grants it to the secular ruler, so that while it can be acknowledged that the power itself is from the pope, the exercise of it is the secular ruler's. These are the words of those who attempt to refute some of the arguments advanced above. There are too some other writers who say that God has given the pope the primary authority of temporal jurisdiction, but not its exercise. The emperor has the executive power from God, not from the pope. This argument is intended to refute some of what has been said above.

That sort of evasion, however, is completely absurd and it is inconsistent with their own arguments. For if the Church acknowledged the executive power to be the secular ruler's, then the secular prince might judge such exercise of it as fell to the pope and take it away from him. But they do not allow this since they assert that the pope cannot be judged by anyone. If God gave the pope the primary authority of secular power, but not its exercise because this would be inappropriate, how can he accept from a prince what God has judged he cannot or ought not to have? And how does he give him what he gets back from him? Again, if the pope has secular power directly from God and the secular ruler its exercise directly from the pope, then the secular ruler is the minister of the pope, just as the pope is the minister of Christ. But this seems to go against the canon of Scripture. For the Apostle says of the king and prince in Romans 13: 'If thou do that which is evil, fear; for he beareth not the sword in vain. For he is God's minister: an avenger to execute wrath etc.' and again, later: 'Therefore also you pay tribute.' He is the minister of God, then; the Apostle does not say, minister of the pope, but minister of God: 'For in this do they serve him' and the Gloss: 'Serve God'.[36] Again, royal power existed in its own right in both principle and practice before papal power and there were kings before there were any Christians in France. Therefore in neither principle nor practice does the royal power there come from the pope but from God and the people who choose a king either as an individual or as a member of a dynasty, as was in fact done formerly. To say that royal power came first directly from God and afterwards from the pope is quite ludicrous. For this cannot be unless Christ gave to Peter the power of conferring the royal office. But as has been shown, this comes indisputably from God. Hence the Gloss on the text in 1 Peter 2, 'Be ye subject to every creature etc.' says, 'Faith and religion do not upset the laws governing place in society'.[37] On the text of Romans 13, 'Let every soul etc.', Ambrose says in the Gloss: 'Although the faithful, as faithful, form one body in Christ, yet there is a difference in their place in society'.

Further, the argument for the proposition that the pope is the intermediary of the power of lesser bishops and priests would seem to be stronger than any argument that he is the mediate agent of the power of kings. For the prelates of the Church are more immediately dependent on him than are secular rulers. Nevertheless the power of prelates does not come to them from God indirectly

---

[36] Rom. 13.4-6 and *glossa ordinaria*.
[37] 1 Pet. 2.13 and *glossa interlinearis*.

through any papal mediation, but directly and also from
the people who elect them or consent to their election.
For it was not Peter, of whom the pope is successor, who
sent forth the other Apostles whose successors are the
bishops, or the seventy-two disciples whose successors are
priests with pastoral responsibility, but Christ who sent
them himself and not through any intermediary, as is
found in Matthew 10[38] and Luke 10.[39] Neither was it
Peter who breathed on the other Apostles, giving them the
Holy Spirit and the power of forgiving sins, but Christ himself, as is written in John 20.[40] D.21 c. *In Novo*[41] tells
how all received similar and equal power from Christ at
the same time. Paul declares that he did not receive his
apostolate from Peter but from Christ, that is from God
without intermediary: 'Paul, an apostle not of men neither
by man but by Jesus Christ and God the Father' and
later, 'For neither did I receive it of man nor did I learn
it', and further on still, he says that he had not seen
Peter until he went to Jerusalem in order to see him, three
years after his call to preach the Gospel.[42] Therefore the
argument that royal power is derived from the pope in
any way whatsoever is correspondingly less tenable.

It sometimes happens that a person who has power to
perform an action does not do it because of some impedi-
ment. An example may be taken from the power to consecrate. A priest having this power might find himself
debarred from performance of the act because of such

---

[38] Matth. 10.5.
[39] Luke 10.1.
[40] John 20.22.
[41] *Decretum* D.21 c.2.
[42] Gal. 1.1, 12, 17-18.

circumstances as material defect, because he has no bread or because of suspension or because of physical defect, if he has become dumb and cannot pronounce the words of consecration. These are impediments which were not expected when the power itself was granted, for no wise man would confer the order of priesthood on someone he knew to be permanently debarred from priestly action. It seems then that we cannot say that the pope has received the power of the secular sword immediately from God whilst regular use of it is denied to him. For this would be to say that God is more superfluous in his works than is nature, which gives virtue to nothing without the act, because who has the power has also the act as is said in *Concerning sleep and wakefulness*,[43] and this would be to make God less wise than man.

The distinction we are discussing cannot be supported by any canon of Scripture unless perhaps they wish to accept St Bernard's dictum that the pope has the material sword at his behest.[44] But this opinion, which is not in any case of great authority, is certainly more against their case than for it, because Bernard says expressly, as will be quoted later, that the pope has the material sword at his behest, because on the pope's indication that the spiritual good demands it, the emperor ought to exercise secular jurisdiction. If however the emperor is unwilling to act or it seems to him inexpedient to act, there is nothing more the pope can do. Hence he is saying that it is the emperor only, not the pope, who has the material sword at command.

---

[43] Aristotle, *De somno et vigilia* c.1.
[44] Cf. St Bernard, *De consideratione* 4.3.

They might try to support their position with the text of 1 Corinthians 6: 'If therefore you have judgments of things pertaining to this world, set them to judge who are the most despised in the Church'.[45] It might seem that the conclusion to be drawn is that it is for priests to set the despised, that is laymen, to judge secular cases. But this text affords no argument to their case. For the Apostle is not here speaking specifically to clergy or churchmen but he is speaking generally to the faithful in reproving them for appointing the despised, that is, the ignorant, to try secular cases. For thereby the faithful were being forced to have recourse to the judgment of pagans, as if there were no one among the faithful wise enough to act as a judge. This is the sense in which the Gloss explains the words 'set them': 'This is not to be understood as exhortation but as irony, that is, you act in such a way, appointing despised and ignorant people, that the faithful are forced to have recourse to the judgment of pagans; I speak as if to your shame, as if to say there were not among you a single wise person etc.'.[46] Thus the Apostle is wishing the faithful laity to appoint conscientious people to judge secular cases and therefore what he is saying has no relevance to the interpretation we have been discussing.

But let it be granted that he was speaking specifically to churchmen. The text still does not support the conclusion alleged. For he did not intend churchmen to appoint judges in every secular case without qualification, but only where jurisdiction over temporal property has been given to them by the secular ruler. For then ought church-

45 1 Cor. 6.4.
46 1 Cor. 6.4 and *glossa interlinearis*.

men to appoint the despised, that is laity, who will exercise judgment in such matters. Thus they should not themselves act in these affairs, as can be seen from present-day practice, for they place lay stewards in charge. The Apostle does not say, '*when* you have judgment of secular matters' but '*if* you have such judgment', suggesting that such cases ought not to be theirs unless granted or permitted by the lay ruler and then they should be judged by 'the despised', that is to say, lay persons, and that according to the principles and practices of civil law, as Hugh of St Victor says explicitly in his book *Concerning the Sacraments*.[47] These are his words: 'It should be noted that sometimes princes grant temporal possessions to the Church, with right of usage only, whether with or without subjects, and sometimes they grant them with both the right of usage and of authority. They concede the use without the authority when they order that the profit of such property be made over to the Church's use, while not permitting any exercise of jurisdiction over the property itself. Sometimes they confer both the use and the authority together, but jurisdiction may not be exercised either by ecclesiastical persons or over secular causes; the Church may employ ministers, laymen, through whom it will make laws and judgments appropriate to the exercise of secular power according to the principles and practices of the civil law'.

What others used to maintain, namely, that secular rulers have the exercise of power from God, and not from the pope, but not the power itself, is not a reasonable argument for it means that God, either directly or through an inter-

---

[47] Hugh of St Victor, *De sacramentis* 2.2.7 PL 176.420.

mediary, gives to one power without the exercise and to another the exercise without the power or authority. This opinion, however, is not too far from our own at least in that its logic precludes appeal from the secular ruler to the pope.

CHAPTER XI

The arguments put forward by those who maintain the contrary position, that the pope does have jurisdiction over temporalities

It is now necessary to discover what are the foundations on which is rested the case of those who say that priests, especially the pope, have the primary power from which the power of princes is derived.

1. They adduce from the decretal *Solitae*[1] that text where God spoke to the priest Jeremias, referring to priestly not royal descent: 'Behold, I have set thee over the nations and over kingdoms, to root up and to pull down and to waste and to destroy, and to build and to plant'.[2] On this basis it is argued that the pope, supreme in the hierarchy of priestly ranks, has the power to remove and appoint kings.

2. They argue that the Matthew text, 'Whatsoever thou shalt bind upon earth it shall be bound also in heaven: and whatsoever thou shalt loose on earth, it shall be loosed also in heaven',[3] is to be interpreted without qualification of any sort.

3. They cite the text: 'Do you not know that you shall judge angels?'[4] with the gloss: 'How much more things of this world?'

---

[1] *Decretales* 1.33.6.
[2] Jer. 1.10.
[3] Matth. 16.19.
[4] 1 Cor. 6.3.

4. The text in Genesis, 'God made two lights'[5] is interpreted: one light is the sun and this symbolizes the pope; as the sun rules the day, so the pope rules spiritual matters. The other light, the moon, ruling the night and so the emperor or king rules temporal matters. But the moon cannot rule the night except by the light it borrows from the sun. It follows then that the authority of the emperor and of kings in temporal affairs comes to them from the pope.

5. Pope Zachary deposed the king of the Franks, putting his brother Pepin in his place as recorded in *Decretum* 15 q.6 c.3.

6. Pope Nicholas says in *Decretum* D. 22 c.1 that Christ conceded and committed to Peter authority of both heavenly and earthly empire.

7. The emperor takes an oath to the pope, as *Decretum* D. 63 c.33.

8. The pope deposes an emperor, *Decretum* 15 q.6 c.3.

9. And has translated the empire from east to west, as the decretal *Venerabilem*[6] relates.

10. Sometimes the pope legitimizes in both the spiritual and temporal orders, as the decretal *Per venerabilem*[7] tells. Sometimes appeal may lie from a secular judge to the pope, as in *Licet*.[8]

11. The pope has absolved soldiers from their oath and on one occasion released all the Franks from their oath of fidelity, as *Decretum* 15 q.6 c.3 and 1 q.4 c.5.

12. The pope has cognizance of every crime. But it is

[5] Gen. 1.16.
[6] *Decretales* 1.6.34.
[7] *Decretales* 4.17.13.
[8] *Decretales* 2.2.10.

agreed that crime can be committed in temporal matters, as when someone illicitly appropriates for himself what belongs to another. The deduction is obvious.

13. When one prince has done an injury to another in a feudal matter, the injured party may denounce the offender to the pope, in which case the pope has cognizance of a temporal matter.

14. It is said in St Matthew's gospel: 'But if thy brother shall offend against thee etc.' and later, 'And if he will not hear them, tell the Church; and if he will not hear the Church let him be to thee as the heathen and publican.'[9] Therefore the church has unreserved power of judging whenever injuries are denounced to it.

15. The emperor Theodosius ordered and Charlemagne renewed the law, that if someone bringing an action wanted to bring it to the judgment of a bishop it should be directed there without question, along with the testimonies of the litigants, even if the other party is opposed to the judgments of bishops, as the decretal *Novit*[10] records.

16. It is written in Deuteronomy[11] and quoted in *Per venerabilem*: 'If thou perceive that there be among you a hard and doubtful matter in judgment between blood and blood, cause and cause, leprosy and leprosy: and thou see that the words of the judges within thy gates do vary: arise, and go up to the place which the Lord thy God shall choose. And thou shalt come to the priests of the Levitical race, and to the judge that shall be at that time, who will show thee the truth of the judgment. And

[9] Matth. 18.15-17.
[10] *Decretales* 2.1.13.
[11] Deut. 17.8-11.

thou shalt do whatsoever they shall say, that preside in the place, which the Lord shall choose, and thou shalt follow their sentence etc.'

17.   Who can do the greater thing can do the lesser. Since therefore the pope can command in spiritual matters, so he can in temporal matters.

18.   Temporal matters have spiritual matters as their object and sometimes are joined to them. Therefore the pope who has the charge of spiritual affairs has the power of judging and ordering temporal affairs at least in so far as they have reference to the spiritual.

19.   The pope alters and transfers unarranged legacies and also it is his responsibility to make restitutions from the property of the deceased when their creditors are not known. Therefore jurisdiction in temporalities is his.

20.   Some men argue in this way: corporal things are ruled through the spirit and depend on it causally, as can be shown in different ways. For the heavenly bodies are controlled through the angels, and in the same way, in man, the soul rules and directs the body. Thus similarly the spiritual power brings into being the temporal power which in turn depends on it as from a first cause, since the temporal power is established rather for the rule of corporal life. It is this argument which Hugh of St Victor seems to touch on in his *Concerning the Sacraments* when he writes: 'As spiritual life is more worthy than temporal life and the spirit than the body, so does the spiritual power excel the temporal power in honour and dignity'.[12]

---

[12] Hugh of St Victor, *De sacramentis* 2.2.4 PL 176.418.

21. For the spiritual power establishes the earthly power in what it is and has the judgment of it should it do wrong. But the spiritual power was established by God underived from any other power and if it errs it can be judged only by him.

22. For it is written: 'But the spiritual man judgeth all things: and he himself is judged of no man'.[13] Thus the spiritual power established secular power and judges it.

23. They argue the same conclusion from the relative importance of ends. In the ordering of arts the art to which pertains the ultimate and principal end controls the arts concerned with secondary ends. The secular power has for its end or purpose the good of a multitude which is to live according to virtue to which it can come by natural virtue and with what supports it. The spiritual power has for its end the supernatural good of the whole which is eternal life and it directs the community to this. But spiritual life is a better and more important end than any other. Therefore the spiritual power granted to the ministers of the Church is superior to the secular power not merely in dignity but insofar as the one is the cause of the other and directs how it should work.

24. They then go on to deduce from this argument that it is the pope who gives to the prince the laws according to which they exercise or should exercise their jurisdiction, nor can a secular prince receive law from any other source without its being papally approved.

25. They say also that the spiritual power is said to be a royal priesthood because Christ is both king and priest and his vicar has royal and priestly power because it is through

[13] 1 Cor. 2.15.

him that the royal power is set up, ordered, sanctified and blessed.

26. They follow Hugh of St Victor[14] in reading in the Old Testament that it was the priesthood which was the first to be instituted by God and afterwards, on God's command, royal power was appointed through the priesthood. And right up to the present in the Church, it is for the sacerdotal dignity to sanctify royal power with its blessing and form it through its institution.

27. Another of their arguments is drawn from Augustine's *Concerning the City of God* where he says that without true justice a republic cannot be ruled and that there cannot by true justice in a republic when Christ is not its ruler.[15] And so there is no rightful and true republic of the sort the Christian republic ought to be unless governance belongs of right to the pope, Christ's vicar. Thus it is concluded that both jurisdictions are granted directly to the pope by God.

28. Further, they cite Romans 13.1, 'What are from God are arranged in order'; both powers are from God; therefore they are arranged in the order whereby the secular power is mediated through the spiritual and does not come from God directly.

29. Another argument runs on these lines: logic would seem to demand that as there is one church, one Christian people and one mystical body, so there must be a single head directing the members both spiritually and temporally. Therefore, they say, all power in the church, whether spiritual or temporal, springs from the one repository of

[14] *De sacramentis* 2.2.4 PL 176.478.
[15] *De civitate Dei* 2.21 (CSEL 40.5.1.89 ff).

both powers, the pope, successor of Peter and vicar of Christ.

30. Further, they produce in support of their case what Bernard writes in Book 4 of his *To Pope Eugenius*: 'Why do you again try to usurp the sword which once for all you were ordered to sheathe? Yet should anyone deny the sword is yours, he would seem not to have given sufficient heed to the word of the Lord when he said: "Put up thy sword into the scabbard".[16] It is therefore yours and it ought to be unsheathed perhaps at your signal, though not by your hand. Otherwise if it in no way belonged to you, when the spokesman for the Apostles said, "Lo, here are two swords"[17] the Lord would not have replied, "It is enough" but, "There are too many".[18] Both spiritual and temporal swords, therefore, belong to the Church. The latter is to be wielded on behalf of the Church, the former by the Church: the one through the mouth of the priest, the other by the hand of the soldier, but at the priest's signal and the emperor's command'.[19] It appears from this exposition that the pope has each of the two powers in their principal authority immediately from God, although the material sword belongs to the emperor.

31. In addition to the arguments already listed some consideration must be given to those of a certain Henry of Cremona, a doctor, on his own reckoning, of canon law.

---

[16] John 18.11.
[17] Luke 22.38.
[18] I read this and the preceding sentence according to Goldast's edition and Bleienstein's variant reading, since they are much nearer what St Bernard wrote than the readings adopted in either the Leclercq or Bleienstein editions.
[19] *De Consideratione* 4.3.

His first argument is that God ruled the world from its beginning; it was he personally who punished Adam and Eve and Cain. His personal rule lasted until the Flood. After this he ruled through Noah whom he had ordered to construct the ark and command it. Noah, according to this interpretation, was a priest because he built an altar and offered sacrifice to God. Afterwards God ruled through Abraham and the other patriarchs who were priests, offering sacrifice to God. Abraham twice built an altar to the Lord and was called priest as may be read in *Decretum* D. 94 c. 24. Later, God ruled through Moses and Aaron who punished Pharaoh and ruled their people in the desert both spiritually and temporally and these men were priests as is written in the Psalms, 'Moses and Aaron among his priests' etc.[20] It would seem to follow that the priests of the New Law who assuredly are not of less authority than those of the Old must similarly rule both spiritually and temporally.

32. It is argued that to have power over the end includes power over the means by which the end is attained. But temporalities are related to the spiritual as means to end, and the pope has power over the spiritual; the conclusion is obvious. Henry of Cremona argued this logic along the following lines: God charged Peter with the care of souls. The body exists for the service of the soul and is subject to it. Temporalities are for the service of the body and are thus subject to it. Therefore from first to last everything is subject to the pope. And the Apostle would seem to agree when he says: 'For all are

[20] Ps. 98.6.

yours. And you are Christ's. And Christ is God's'.[21] On
which the Gloss comments (though Henry failed to make
use of this authority for his own case): 'Everything whatsoever which is in the world is yours'.

33.   Henry of Cremona argues also that even if emperors
had had any right in the empire from the beginning, they
forfeited it because of the sins they committed in killing
the saints and especially popes and their right was transferred to the pope because he who abuses a liberty granted
to him deserves to lose his privilege, as is said in the
Decretum 11 q.3 c.63.

34.   He also argues that the power which the church now
has and which it used not to have was prefigured in
chapter 14 of St Luke's gospel. The reference is to the
parable of the man who sent his servant at the hour of
supper to tell the guests that they should come; which
done, the servant was ordered to go out into the highways
and hedges and compel them to come in that his house
might be filled.[22] The significance of the parable is that it
shows how initially the church had no powers of compul-
sion because it was itself subject. But now in its modern
state it has full authority to compel and command everyone
as Augustine says, *Decretum* 23 q.4 c.38. Other men
draw similar conclusions from Psalm 2: 'Why have the
Gentiles raged'. They say that this first hostility to Christ
of pagans and Jews signifies the state of the primitive
church. Later it is said: 'Let us break their bonds asunder:
let us cast away their yoke from us', and 'And now, o
ye kings understand: receive instruction you that judge the

21 1 Cor. 3.22-3.
22 Luke 14.17, 23.

earth' and, 'Embrace discipline', etc.[23] These verses signify the church of recent times when the pope, vicar of Christ, has power over the kings of earth who are wholly subject to him although he did not have this power from the beginning. Some men point the contrast between the Lord's conversion of the first of the Apostles, Peter and Andrew, by simple call, with the violent fall which attended the conversion of Paul, the last of them, and adapt the contrast to make the same sort of point as has been made from the texts already mentioned.

35. They argue further to the diminution of royal power and the elevation of papal dignity, that God established a priesthood right from the beginning of the history of his chosen people. But he did not institute a king, merely leaving the decision to their wish, as in Deuteronomy: 'When thou shalt say: I will set a king over me' etc.[24] And it was an angry Lord who gave them permission to have a king as appears from what he said to Samuel: 'They have not rejected thee, but me, that I should not reign over them'.[25] From this it appears that God did not accept royal government so much as suffer it to exist, and that it is more acceptable to God that the world be ruled by one priest in all matters. Hence it is written concerning kings: 'They have reigned, but not by me: they have been princes and I knew not'.[26]

36. To belittle further royal power and prove papal rule over temporalities, they have recourse to the Genesis

[23] Ps. 2.1, 3, 10, 12.
[24] Deut. 17.14.
[25] 1 Kings 8.7.
[26] Os. 8.4.

account of the famine in Egypt and of how Pharaoh bought the land of all the Egyptians, and during this famine subjected the priests to his service, so managing their needs that they were not deprived either of possessions or of freedom, as though the lord deemed that among all peoples priests henceforth should be free.[27] The same argument is used by Pope Urban in *Decretum* 23 q.8 c.22 to show that it appears that clerical property should not be subject to imperial exactions.

37. Should the pope order the bishops of any region to present themselves at the curia and the king from whom they hold fiefs say that he needs the presence of those bishops and that they must stay, they must obey the pope. At least, then, in this case bishops are not subject to the prince for it would seem that the pope has exempted them. The source of this argument is *Decretum* 23 q.8 c.19.

38. They say that the pope can deprive kings of that customary right of patronage by which they collate to prebends. The reasons they put forward for this opinion are: because collation to benefices is to some degree spiritual or connected with the spiritual just as is the right to tithe, and therefore does not belong to a layman; because the dowry of the church should not carry burdens; because custom cannot overrule public law according to which disposition of ecclesiastical benefices belongs to the ordinary, not to any lay person; because a condition or custom which is wrong in itself or contrary to the substance of a contract is inapplicable, and lay collation is a wrong custom and therefore inapplicable; because the church has in law the standing of a minor and therefore

[27] Gen. 47.13 ff.

when it accounts itself injured by such agreements and dissimulations it can demand retribution in full. So the pope, acting for the Church, can demand its right in this matter and inhibit kings from continuing to confer ecclesiastical benefices.

39. To confirm their opinion, they argue that the pope must be self-sufficient as regards both types of religious life, active and contemplative, much more so than any other prelate. But he cannot be self-sufficient for the active life unless he has direct and meaningful power over temporalities because administration of temporalities belongs to the active life.

40. Again they say that the clergy are more vigorous in reasoning and intellect than the laity and therefore ought to have the leadership in both.

41. They assert that those who take a view contrary to their own are really speaking on behalf of princes in expectation of gain or through fear and not according to conscience.

42. Finally, Henry of Cremona says that those who will not allow that the pope has everywhere power in temporalities should be judged as heretics since they are saying in effect that the Church cannot coerce heretics with the help of the secular arm.

These are the relevant arguments I have heard and have been able to collect.

CHAPTER XII

Some general ideas preliminary both to the repudiation of the arguments of the preceding chapter and to the proper understanding of that authority which Christ has given to the pope in temporal matters. The powers given by Christ to Peter and the Apostles are considered first

For a clear solution of these problems, one must decide first what kind of power the Apostles and disciples of the Lord, and through them the bishops and priests, received from Christ. For as the Gloss on Luke 10 says, just as the Apostles provide a model for the episcopate, so the seventy-two disciples provide a model for the priesthood of second rank, and all sacerdotal power is concentrated in these two ranks.

What was shown in chapter 2 above must be remembered, namely, that the priesthood is nothing other than a spiritual power conferred on ministers of the Church to dispense to the faithful those grace-bearing sacraments by which we are conducted towards eternal life. Nature does not fall short in what is essential; when it gives a power, it gives it only with all aids sufficient to the proper exercise of that power in the manner appropriate for its operation. Hence the Philosopher argues[1] that it would be unnatural for nature to give a certain power of the soul to

---

[1] Cf. Aristotle, *De generatione animalium* c.1.

anyone and not the organs necessary for the fulfilment of the soul's operation. So therefore, when God, who is more perfect than nature, gives spiritual power to priests, he gives them those means necessary for its proper execution. There are five such means, without which spiritual power cannot be properly exercised.

The first concerns the sacraments, namely, the sanctification and consecration of the physical material itself, for according to both Hugh[2] and the Master of the Sentences,[3] a sacrament is an element perceptible to the senses, sanctified and consecrated through the word of God. Two more concern the faithful to whom the sacraments are administered: the first of these is correct instruction and knowledge through doctrine, so that they know how they ought to live in order to receive the sacraments worthily, because they are only conferred on those in the proper dispositions; the other is the coercion of those who despise the sacraments, so that those who cannot be persuaded from evil through realization of the vileness that is in sin or through warnings and salutary advice, may be frightened away from it through fear of legal punishment. A further two concern the ministers of the sacraments: two things are required for them. The first is their due differentiation and orderly arrangement. For if the great mass of ministers is not ordered or differentiated by some authority with power to do this, there would be confusion, and neglect of the common good would follow if each minister were able to exercise his jurisdiction anywhere,

[2] Hugh of St Victor, *De sacramentis* 1.9.2.
[3] Peter Lombard, *Sententiae* 4.d.1. c.2-4.

for men are not usually so solicitous for the common good as they are for their own. There would be occasion for dissension both among the faithful and between ministers, if all ministers were to have pastoral responsibility over all people without any formal organization, as was the case in the early Church when one could say: 'I belong to Paul' and another, 'I belong to Apollo'.[4] It is therefore necessary to have organization of ministers imposed by one who has the requisite authority. The second means concerning ministers of the sacraments, fifth and last of the means without which priestly power could not be exercised, is provision of what is necessary for the support of life.

According to the Gospel, six powers were granted to the Apostles and disciples of the Lord and so therefore, to their successors, the ministers of the Church. One is that power of consecration, sometimes called the character or power of order, which the Lord gave to his disciples at the Last Supper when, in giving them his body in the form of bread, he bade them: 'Do this in remembrance of me'.[5] Another is the power of administering the sacraments and especially the sacrament of penance, which is the power of the keys or of spiritual jurisdiction in the sphere of conscience, consisting in the authority of judging between leprosy and non-leprosy,[6] in the power of absolving from guilt and changing the condition of the guilty from deserving the punishment of eternal damnation to being punishable by temporal punishment. This power in the spiritual forum was promised to Peter as Matthew says,

[4] 1 Cor. 1.12.
[5] Luke 22.19.
[6] Cf. Deut. 17.8.

'I will give you the keys etc. ...'[7] and in Matthew 18 where it was promised to all: 'Truly, I say to you, whatever you bind on earth etc. ...'[8] It was actually given to them when it was said to them in John 20: '"As the Father has sent me, even so I send you". And when he had said this, he breathed on them and said to them, "Receive the Holy Spirit. If you forgive the sins of any, they are forgiven etc."'.[9] In some people's opinion, this power of administering the sacraments is the same in essence as the power of consecration, though differing according to the different ways it is used in respect of the body of Christ, true or mystical, and this is the completion of the sacerdotal power. Hence in the ordination of mere priests and also of bishops, who are high priests, the same words are pronounced, namely, those already mentioned above: 'Receive the Holy Spirit. If you forgive etc.'

The third power is the authority of the apostolate or of preaching which the Lord gave them, as is recounted in Matthew 10 when he said, 'And preach as you go, saying "the kingdom of heaven is at hand"',[10] and in the last chapter of Matthew: 'Go therefore and make disciples of all nations'.[11]

The fourth power is judicial, that power to coerce in the external forum by which sins are corrected through fear of punishment, especially sins in scandal of the Church. The concession of this power is in Matthew 18: 'If thy brother shall offend against thee etc. ... If he will not

---

[7] Matth. 16.19.
[8] Matth. 18.18.
[9] John 20.21-23.
[10] Matth. 10.7.
[11] Matth. 28.19.

hear them, tell the Church; and if he will not hear the Church let him be to thee as the heathen and publican.' The Gloss comments here: 'In order that the reproach of many might correct him' and there follows in Matthew: 'Truly, I say to you whatever you bind etc.' and the Gloss: 'The authority to judge in this forum has been given to the Church when it is said: "Tell the Church", that is, so that it might have cognizance, and also the authority to coerce or punish through ecclesiastical censure when it is said: "If he will not hear the Church, let him be to thee as the heathen, etc."'. The confirmation of this is added with the words: 'Truly I say to you whatever you bind etc.' and the Gloss: 'By the bond of anathema'.[12] It is especially to be reflected upon that in these three acts, illumination through doctrine, purification through correction, perfection through the sacraments, priests have the full power of priestly rule over the community of the faithful.

The fifth is the power, according to the opinion of some, of distributing ministers by establishing ecclesiastical jurisdictions, so that confusion be avoided. This power was granted to Peter and his successors in virtue of what was said to him: 'Feed my sheep'.[13] For the power of the keys and the power of jurisdiction were given to all equally without establishing boundaries and each could use it effectively on any sinner at all, since the sinner is the proper subject on which the action of the jurisdiction, the absolution, falls, in the same way as wheaten bread, without qualification, is the matter on which falls the exercise of the power of order. Thus it was that St Paul

[12] Matth. 18.15-18 and *Glossa interlinearis*.
[13] John 21.17.

exercised his priestly rule over the people uncircumscribed by any boundaries, as is obvious to anyone who examines his letters. Because, as has been said already, confusion could have arisen from this state of affairs, the Lord in his foresight granted to Peter and his successors the authority to distribute ministers of the Church and determine their jurisdictional boundaries, when he said: 'Feed my sheep', implying that there was a general shepherd to whom belongs the organization and general administration of sheep and sheepfold. This command was not given to any other apostle. Some say, and with reason, that it is not any sinner without qualification who is matter for the effective exercise of the keys or power of jurisdiction, but the sinner as subject to a particular authority; therefore the power in question has no effect except in the context of that subjection, which makes a man proper matter for the valid exercise of the power in the same way as the power of order has no validity except on wheaten bread. It is this jurisdiction or supreme prelacy over the whole Church, which was given to Peter, by subjecting the faithful to him, when he was told: 'Feed my sheep', that is, 'Be shepherd and prelate, and I commit and subject the Church to you as shepherd'. Thus Theophilus: 'The meal over, he committed the care of the sheep to Peter and to no other person'. Gregory says very much the same.[14] So, therefore, although all the Apostles received the same power from Christ, an equal power of the keys and spiritual jurisdiction, yet it was Peter alone and whoever on whom he wished to confer it who received the power of jurisdiction and its subject matter. In this reading 'Feed my sheep' does not

---

[14] Cf. Aquinas, *Catena aurea in Johannem* c.21.

mean that Peter was given a power, already held by all the Apostles, of regulating jurisdiction, but that jurisdiction was given in the first place to Peter alone and afterwards he distributed it in parts, calling others to a share of the pastoral charge.

According to the first opinion, however, the explanation of why no bishop might absolve outside his own diocese lies in the decision made by Peter, or by the authority of the Church, to establish and prohibit; for without express prohibition, a bishop could otherwise do so and even still, should he do so, what he did would be valid, since he has the power in his own right and there is proper subject matter, namely the sinner. He would, however, be acting wrongly in transgressing the rule of the Church, just as a member of the Latin rite, speaking the words of consecration over leavened bread would validly consecrate, though he would commit sin in doing so through violating that rule of the Church which ordered him to use unleavened bread. This interpretation harmonizes with the position in respect of the right of ownership of private property. Just as acquisition of property is permissible only because of decision made by men and if this were rescinded I would not be able to say 'This is mine', for all things are in common, so if the rule of the Church were withdrawn, a particular community would no more belong to any one bishop than to any other and absolution could be obtained quite unrestrictedly from any priest at all. Particular allocation has been made by the Church on the authority granted to Peter in the command: 'Feed my sheep'.

According to the second opinion, the rule that a bishop should not absolve outside his own diocese does not derive so much from any rule of the Church as from material defect. Outside his own diocese, there is no community subject to him, so that his intention to absolve and his pronunciation of the words of absolution over a sinner will not absolve him, any more than a priest who pronounces the words of consecration over a stone or over bread other than wheaten, accomplishes a valid consecration.

There are those who maintain a third opinion, namely that the words 'Feed my sheep' conferred on Peter only that authority to teach and construct, which belongs to prelates, while the exercise of that authority was commanded of them in the injunction, 'Go, teach etc.'; hence the Gloss: 'Feed my sheep, by word, example and with bodily nourishment'.[15]

The sixth power would seem to spring logically from all the foregoing. It is the power to receive what is necessary to maintain a suitable standard of living from those to whom they minister spiritually. This power was given to Peter and the Apostles and declared obligatory when, in Matthew 10, after Christ had bade them go out and preach, he added instruction as to how they should conduct themselves towards temporal possessions: 'You received without pay, give without pay' and the Gloss: 'Just as I give you such power without pay, do you also give freely lest the grace of the gospel be corrupted'; and again in the text: 'Take no gold, nor silver, nor copper in your belts', Gloss: 'You who exhort others to despise riches'; and again in the text, 'No bag for your journey, nor two tunics, nor sandals, nor a staff', Gloss: 'He

---

[15] Aquinas, *ibid.*

deprives them of the near necessity of the help of a stick lest they who teach that all things are ruled by God should take heed for the morrow'. The text goes on about their power to accept: 'For the labourer deserves his food', Gloss: 'See here why he ordered them to carry nothing, since all is their due',[16] and elsewhere in the Gloss: 'Receive necessities only in so far as they satisfy need and then, untroubled in mind, you will be the freer for what is eternal'.[17] More is said concerning this power to accept what is necessary for livelihood in the last chapter of St Matthew and in Luke 10.

These six then, are the powers which the Apostles received from Christ. They received no other except that of working miracles to confirm faith. There is no necessity for bishops and priests to follow them here, for the confirmation of our faith is so manifest as no longer to need confirmation by miracles.

---

[16] Matth. 10.8-10 and *Glossa interlinearis*.
[17] *Glossa ordinaria ad Matth.* 5.

CHAPTER XIII

Prelates of the Church have neither lordship nor jurisdiction in temporal affairs by virtue of the powers granted to them nor on their account are princes subject to them in temporal affairs

Having examined the powers given to bishops and priests, it is now necessary to examine what of temporal relevance has been granted to them with those powers. It would seem that none of them confers any direct temporal power or jurisdiction, except that clergy may accept what is necessary for support of life. Let us examine each of these powers in turn.

The first is the power to consecrate. It is self-evident that this is a wholly spiritual matter and that it is possessed equally by all bishops and priests even by those who have been degraded, suspended or deposed, as is shown in the fact that when they are reconciled to the Church they are not reordained. It is obvious that they derive nothing of temporal jurisdiction or lordship from this power.

The second power is that of the keys in the sphere of conscience. This too is wholly spiritual: Chrysostom commenting on John 22, 'Receive the Holy Spirit etc.'[1] says, 'The spiritual power was granted to them only for the forgiveness of sins'.[2] The pope gets no authority in

---

[1] John 20.22.
[2] Aquinas, *Catena aurea in Io.* 20.22.

temporal affairs from this power except when, in the sphere of conscience, he persuades the penitent to make satisfaction, imposing this as he imposes other penances, even corporal ones. Yet no one becomes hereby subject to him in any unqualified sense, but under conditions, namely if he sins and wishes to do penance. If a person should not wish to do penance, then the pope cannot compel him because of the power of the keys as a secular prince can compel a culprit by fine or other correction imposed and enforced even on one unwilling to accept punishment.

The third power or authority is that of preaching. This is entirely spiritual and the pope has no lordship because of it, since it is not in itself a power to command, but an authority to teach, as the Apostle says in 1 Timothy 2: 'For this I was appointed a preacher and apostle, a teacher of the Gentiles in faith and truth'.[3] Further, Bernard, *To Eugenius*: 'Tyranny is forbidden to apostles and apostolic men' and again: 'You shall tame the wolves and shall not tyrannize over the sheep'.[4] And again, the Apostle Peter: 'Not as domineering over those in your charge but being examples to the flock'.[5] There is however an indirect power in temporal affairs connected with this authority to teach, in that priests persuade men to penances and restitution of the money of others and disposal of temporal goods as the order of charity demands.

The nub of the difficulty lies in the fourth power, that of judgment in the external forum. It must be appre-

---

[3] 1 Tim. 2.7.
[4] *De consideratione* 2.6.
[5] 1 Pet. 5.3.

ciated that there are two facets of this power. The first
is that authority to judge and settle cases which is in-
dicated in the text: 'Tell the Church'.[6] The other is the
power to coerce, spoken as in the text: 'Let him be to thee
as a heathen etc.'[7] These are the two keys of the external
forum. About the first of them it must be understood
that the ecclesiastical judge, in so far as he is an ecclesiastic,
has no regular cognizance of anything in the external forum
except for spiritual cases which are called ecclesiastical,
and none at all in temporal cases, save for reason of sin.
If, however, the nature of the sin is well understood, it
is not proper to make an exception even of this case,
since the Church does not have cognizance of sin except
in so far as it is brought into the spiritual and ecclesiastical
sphere. Sin can be committed in temporal matters in two
ways. One way is by sin of belief or error; for example,
if a man thinks that usury is no mortal sin or when in
property matters there is doubt as to the legality in God's
eyes of the titles by which he holds or sells. Since it is
the divine law which rules on such questions and it is by
this law that the ecclesiastical judge must frame his
judgments, there can be no doubt that legal process
concerning them is for the ecclesiastical judge only. The
other way of committing sin in relation to temporal property, is in aiming to secure another's property for oneself or making threats to do so. Cognizance of such
matters belongs to the civil judge only and he judges
according to those human civil laws which regulate the
buying and selling of property in order to ensure that

[6] Matth. 18.17.
[7] *Ibid.*

property is put to those proper human uses which would
be neglected if everyone held everything in common. For
if things were held unreservedly in common, it would not
be easy to keep the peace among men. It was for this
reason that private possession of property was introduced
by the emperors, as Augustine says in his commentary on
St John's Gospel reproduced in D. 8 c. *Quo iure*:[8] 'Take
away the laws of emperors and you are not then able to
say, this thing is mine. For in natural law there is equal
freedom and common possession for everyone in everything.' It is not therefore for the ecclesiastical judge to
judge of sin in temporalities but for the secular judge
only, unless perhaps Christ conceded and allowed it to the
ecclesiastical judge in some other way.

Bernard made reference to this in his *To Pope Eugenius*:
'Your power is not in possessions but in hearts',[9] as noticed
above and in chapter 10. Further, on Matthew 18 'That
every word may be confirmed by the evidence of two or
three witnesses', the Gloss explains: 'So that you may
prove it to be sinful if he has denied that it is so. For if
he does not agree with them, then must he be denounced
to the Church and not elsewhere, for the Church judges
concerning sin'.[10] Again, in D. 96 c. *Duo sunt* the pope
addresses the emperor: 'Know that you are subject in such
matters to their judgment', that is, to the judgment of
priests and the Gloss explains: 'As to spiritual matters'.[11]
Popes have enunciated the same principle in the following

[8] *Decretum* D.8 c.1.
[9] *De consideratione* 1.6.
[10] Matth. 18.16; Aquinas, *Catena aurea in Matthaeum* c.18.
[11] *Decretum* D.96 c.10 and *glossa ordinaria*.

decretals: *Extra. Qui filii sint legitimi c. Lator,*[12] which states that the secular judge or lord should have judgment of hereditary right and *c. Causam*[13] of the same title, which says: 'We take account of the fact that it is for the king to judge of such property matters, not the Church, lest we should appear to detract from the right of the king of England who claims that such judgment belongs to him'; *Extra. De iudiciis c. Novit:*[14] 'We have no intention of judging a feudal issue which is of the king's jurisdiction, unless exceptionally etc.'; *Extra. De appellationibus c. Si duobus*[15] rules that no appeal lies from the secular judge to the pope except in territory subject or granted to the Church. To say that popes teach and write this doctrine merely from humility is completely dangerous and is 'to set the mouth against heaven';[16] the Philosopher in *Ethics IV*[17] classifies this as the vice of irony opposed to truth, saying that people who profess this sort of humility are not virtuous but fainthearted and self-deceivers. Augustine says in his book *On the words of the Apostle*: 'When you lie for the sake of humility, if you were not a sinner before you lied, you make yourself one by lying'[18] and similarly, *On St John's Gospel*: 'Not thus is arrogance guarded against, by abandoning truth'.[19] Gregory says: 'Imprudent are the humble who ensnare themselves in lying'.[20]

---

[12] *Decretales* 4.17.5.
[13] *Decretales* 4.17.7.
[14] *Decretales* 2.1.13.
[15] *Decretales* 2.28.7.
[16] Cf. Psalms 72.9.
[17] Aristotle, *Nic. Ethics* 4.7.
[18] *Sermo* 181 c.4 PL 38.981.
[19] *In Iohannem* tract. 43 PL 35.1712.
[20] Gregory the Great, *Moralia* 5.26.5.

In the matter of the power of correction or ecclesiastical
censure, it should be appreciated that its relevance is purely spiritual, for it can impose no penalty in the external
forum save only a spiritual one, except it be conditionally
and incidentally. It is for the ecclesiastical judge to lead
men back to God, preventing them from sinning and
correcting them; this function is exercised in the way God
had laid down, which is that of excluding sinners from
the sacraments and from the community of the faithful and
the other penalties appropriate to ecclesiastical coercion.
In saying that temporal punishments might only be imposed 'conditionally', I mean on the condition that the
sinner wishes to repent and to accept money penance.
For an ecclesiastical judge cannot, for reason of sin, impose a corporal or money penalty as can a secular judge,
except on the condition that the guilty party is willing
to accept it. Should he not be willing to accept it, then the
ecclesiastical judge coerces him by excommunication or
other spiritual penalty, which is the very most he can
inflict; he can impose nothing beyond that. I also said
'incidentally', because if a ruler were an incorrigible heretic
and despises ecclesiastical sanctions, the pope might take
such action with the people as would lead them to deprive
him of office and to depose him. The pope might do this
in a case of ecclesiastical crime of which the cognizance
is his, by excommunicating all who continued to obey him
as their ruler. Thus it would be the people who actually
deposed him, with the pope acting 'incidentally'. Conversely, if the pope were an incorrigible criminal, a cause
of scandal to the Church, a secular ruler might indirectly
bring about his excommunication and deposition, by warn-
ing him, personally or through the cardinals. Should the

pope refuse to submit, the ruler might take such action
with the people as would force the pope to resign or be
deposed by the people. For the emperor could prevent each
and everyone from obeying such a pope or serving him as
such, by taking securities or imposing corporal penalties.
Thus each can take action against the other, for both the
pope and emperor have universal jurisdiction, though the
one has spiritual jurisdiction and the other temporal.

A distinction must be made here. Where a king offends
in spiritual matters like faith and marriage and the other
categories of offences which fall to the ecclesiastical jurisdiction, the pope's first action should be to admonish him.
If the offender persists in his conduct and proves incorrigible, he should then be excommunicated. But the
pope may inflict no further penalties, as was said, except
incidentally by acting with the people after the guilty party
has despised ecclesiastical correction. Where, however, the
king offends in those temporal matters of which cognizance
is not ecclesiastical, then the initiative in starting the
corrective process is not the pope's but belongs to the
barons and peers of the kingdom. If they cannot act, or
dare not, they can ask for the help of the Church and
the Church, on this request from the peers to uphold the
law, can admonish the prince and proceed against him according to the procedure already described.

A similar principle applies should a pope commit a
temporal offence, cognizance of which belongs to the
secular ruler, as for example, if he lend at usury or
protect usurers and especially if he does what the civil law
forbids. In such a case, it would fall to the emperor, if
there were one, as having primary right, to correct by
admonition and punishment, for it is to the prince that

belongs primary right of correcting all evil-doers: 'For he beareth not the sword in vain. For he is God's minister: an avenger to execute wrath upon him that doth evil'.[21] And the Gloss on 'For therefore also you pay tribute' comments, 'Because for this are they instituted that the good be praised and the evil be punished'.[22] Similarly Jerome on Jeremias as cited in 23.q.5:[23] 'The proper function of a king is to execute judgment and justice and deliver him who is oppressed out of the hand of the oppressor and also foreigners and orphans and widows who are more easily oppressed by the strong'. Hence the Emperor Henry praiseworthily deposed two rival candidates for the papacy not only by canonical but also by imperial censure, as may be read in the *Chronicle of the Romans*.[24] I say that the emperor has primary right to correct the pope without any intermediary for any crime, particularly civil ones, because there is a privilege that clerics should be judged only by their bishops. But this privilege was granted by princes and began when, in the life time of Constantine, it was obtained by Julius, second pope after Sylvester, as is related in the *Chronicles*.[25] Some, however, maintain that the privilege is founded on divine law and not on any concession granted by princes, according to the saying of the Psalms: 'Touch ye not my anointed'.[26] which they interpret as referring to priests. Others, however, interpret it as referring to kings who were at that time anoin-

---

[21] Rom. 13.4.
[22] Rom. 13.6 and *glossa ordinaria*.
[23] *Decretum* 23 q.5 c.23.
[24] Cf. Vincent of Beauvais, *Speculum historiale*.
[25] *Op. cit.* 13.57.
[26] Ps. 104.15.

ted, as stated in 1 Kings when it is reported that David slew Doech because he said he had slain the Lord's anointed, namely Saul.[27]

If, however, a pope were delinquent in spiritual matters, for example, in conferring benefices simoniacally or squandering church property or depriving churchmen and chapters of their rights or by false profession or teaching in matters touching faith and morals, then he ought first to be warned by the cardinals who stand in the place of the whole clergy. Should he prove incorrigible and the cardinals cannot on their own remove this scandal from the Church, then they may have recourse to the secular arm to support the rule of law. Then the emperor, as a member of the Church, at the request of the cardinals, should proceed against him to accomplish his deposition. For this is the manner that the Church holds the secular sword, not indeed to wield of itself or at its command but at its signal and entreaty, as Bernard told Eugenius.[28] For this is the way two swords are bound to lend help to each other in that common charity which united the members of the Church. This principle can be deduced from D.96 c. Cum ad verum,[29] 23 q. 5 c. Principes seculi[30] and the canons following. It is told in the Chronicles[31] how Constantine II through ambition had frequently given scandal to the Church, was deposed by the princes, and by the zeal of the faithful had his eyes put out. Similarly John XII, a wanton, devoted to the chase, frequently warned as to his conduct and

[27] Cf. 2 Kings 1.16.
[28] De consideratione 4.3.
[29] Decretum D.96 c.6.
[30] Decretum 23 q.5 c.20; Jer. 22.3.
[31] Cf. Vincent of Beauvais, Speculum historiale 23.167.

failing to correct himself, was deposed by the emperor and clergy and Pope Leo took his place though he was still alive.[32] So too it is related how, when the priests had received offerings from the people for repairs to the buildings of the temple and had failed to carry them out, King Joas forbade them to take any further offerings, sent his own men to receive the money and so the temple buildings were repaired and the money paid out to the workmen.[33]

The foregoing arguments establish the principle that all ecclesiastical sanction is spiritual, consisting of excommunication, suspension and interdict; other than this, the Church can do nothing except indirectly and incidentally, as has already been said. That all ecclesiastical jurisdiction is spiritual is shown from what is said in Matthew 18: 'If he will not hear the Church: let him be to thee as the heathen and publican', Gloss: 'So that the reprimand of many may correct him'.[34] And there follows: 'Truly I say to you, whatever you bind etc.', Gloss: 'By the bond of anathema'.[35] Chrysostom says on the same text: 'See how he binds the incorrigible with a double fate, namely the penalty suffered here, ejection from the Church, which he has noted when he said "Let him be to thee as the heathen and publican" and the future penalty, which is to be bound in heaven, so that in a multitude of judgments the fault of a brother may be corrected'.[36] This is the opinion of the Apostle, 1 Corinthians 5: 'If any man

---

[32] Cf. *op. cit.* 24.86.
[33] Cf. 4 Kings 12.7-15.
[34] Matth. 18.17 and *glossa interlinearis*.
[35] Matth. 18.18 and *glossa interlinearis*.
[36] Cf. Aquinas, *Catena aurea in Matthaeum* c.18.

that is named a brother among you be a fornicator or a drunkard or an extortioner: with such a one, not so much as to eat'.[37] Notice how the Apostle does not go beyond excommunication even for serious faults and instructed all bishops: 'A man that is a heretic after the first and second admonition, avoid: knowing that he that is such a one is subverted'.[38] Note that he does not say 'Burn' but 'Avoid'. From these texts it is clear that the power is a spiritual one and princes are not subject to it, except in the way already explained. The power granted to Peter in the words 'Feed my sheep'[39] is to be understood in the same sense, namely that it is spiritual only and grants no power over princes however it is interpreted in the first, second or third ways.

The sixth power, that of receiving what is necessary for due sustenance of life, is a temporal one. It ought rather to be described as a certain right owed to them as stipend for their maintenance, in relation to which princes are not subjects but only debtors, in just the same way as are all others of the faithful who receive spiritual benefits from them. This right was owed to the Apostles but they did not demand it with the voice of authority, but with that of humble entreaty. However, the pope may pronounce this to be due to them and to be legally claimable as possessions and even, under ecclesiastical sanction, to force the rebellious to render what is owed.

[37] 1 Cor. 5.11.
[38] Tit. 3.11.
[39] John 21.17.

CHAPTER XIV

Replies to the first set of six arguments

1. To the interpretation of the Jeremias text, 'Behold I have set thee over the nations and over kingdoms etc.', I reply that this text can be interpreted in a twofold way. Some argue that since the name Jeremias means exalted of the Lord, the person addressed is Christ.[1] For in the same way, many things were said of Solomon which were fulfilled in Christ, who was thus prefigured in Solomon, as Augustine shows in his *City of God,* chapter 17.[2] But Christ thus prefigured in Jeremias, as one set over the nations and kingdoms of the world, when shown them from a mountain top and offered them as gifts from the devil, rejected them with scorn.[3] Or again, the reading is that he is set over them as head over the members of his body, who in remaining loyal to him have overcome the cruelty of kings and kingdoms by patience, armed with the constancy of faith as in 'Who through faith conquered kingdoms'[4] and Solomon's saying, 'The patient man is better than the valiant'.[5] If the text be read as referring to the person of Jeremias, it would be agreed that he never for any reason at all deposed any king from his throne and his being set over nations and kingdoms should

---

[1] Jer. 1.10 and *glossa ordinaria.*
[2] *De civitate Dei* 17.20 (CSEL 40.5.2. 257 ff).
[3] Cf. Matth. 4.8.
[4] Heb. 11.33.
[5] Prov. 16.32.

be interpreted as having authority over them to proclaim
the truth, in the same way as the Psalm speaks of David
and Christ: 'But I am appointed king by him over Sion,
his holy mountain, preaching his commandment';[6] he was
set over nations and kingdoms in conquering them in
patience, as he took in his hand the cup of pure wine
with orders to give all nations to drink. So therefore the
text goes on: 'To root up', Gloss: 'Evils'; 'And to pull
down and to waste', Interlinear Gloss: 'The kingdoms
of the devil'; 'and to build', Interlinear Gloss: 'You shall
not scandalize the Church'; 'and to plant', Interlinear
Gloss: 'Good things'. Thus the text in the sense expounded by the saint has no relevance to the deposition and
destruction of kings of earth and the creation of others
in their place, but refers to the rooting out of vices and
the planting of true faith and morals, in the sense of that
passage of 1 Corinthians 3: 'You are God's field, God's
building'.[7] Therefore the text is said to have been about
priests not of kings, for this work is not done by royal and
secular power but by spiritual power. It is also said to
refer to the priests who were in Anathoth, which is to
be interpreted as 'the answer' because priests do this
work rather by answering concerning faith and morals than
by domination of the secular power. Thus the text we are
discussing is preceded by the words, 'The Lord touched his
mouth and gave his words in it',[8] because priests fulfil
their duties more by mouth and doctrine, as teachers, than
by hand and power, as lords. This interpretation is con-

[6] Ps. 2.6.
[7] 1 Cor. 3.9.
[8] Jer. 1.9.

firmed by Bernard when in Book 2 of *To Pope Eugenius,* he speaks of the nature of papal rulership: 'Gird yourself with your sword which is the sword of the spirit, the word of God' and later: 'Thus shall you tame the wolves and not tyrannize the sheep'.[9]

2. The argument based on, 'Whatsoever thou shalt bind on earth etc.'.[10]

In the view of Chrysostom and Rabanus, nothing was given here other than spiritual power — power, that is to say, to absolve from the bonds of sin.[11] It would be stupid to deduce from this text that any power to absolve from the bond of debts was given. Moreover, according to Jerome, this power should not be understood as having effect if the key is defective. Thus he says that some priests and bishops not understanding that statement have imitated the arrogance of the Pharisees in thinking they can condemn the innocent or loose the guilty. But with God it is not the sentence of priests but the way of life of the accused which counts. Jerome illustrated this with an example he took from the priests of the old law who by virtue of their office were not cleansing, or making the unclean clean, but rather were judging the clean and the unclean.[12] Richard of St Victor in his book *On the Forgiveness of Sins,* chapter 11 explains the text we are examining thus: 'The Lord did not say: "Whatever you wish to bind and loose" but "Whatever you bind and

---

[9] *De consideratione* 2.6.
[10] Matth. 16.19.
[11] *Glossa ordinaria in Matth.* 16; Rabanus Maurus, *Commentarium in Matth.* c.16.
[12] *Glossa ordinaria, loc. cit.*

loose". It is therefore the just not the unjust sentence of priests that binds and looses'.[13]

3. The argument based on the text, 'Do you not know that you shall judge angels?'[14] According to Ambrose and the venerable exegetes, the Apostle is not speaking here specifically to the clergy but generally to all the faithful who tended to choose pagan judges in secular cases to the scandal of our faith, as if there were no wise men among the faithful capable of acting as judges, and this he rightly rebuked.[15]

4. The argument based on the text 'God made two great lights etc.'.[16]

I reply that this is a mystical exposition of the text, and according to Denis a mystical reading cannot be accepted unless a proof in found from some other passage of Scripture, because mystical exegesis does not proceed by proof.[17] Moreover, this particular mystical interpretation is not that given by the saints; their reading tended the other way. Isidore says in the Gloss on Genesis that 'the sun' is to be understood as 'kingdom' and 'the moon' as 'priesthood'. Hence he says: 'The splendour of the sun represents the excellence of the kingdom, and people obedient to their king; the splendour of the moon is as a representation of the synagogue; the stars are the princes, and all things are rooted in the stability of the kingdom as in a firm foundation'.[18] But let our opponents' inter-

---

[13] Richard of St Victor, *De potestate ligandi et solvendi* c.11. PL 196.1167.
[14] 1 Cor. 6.3.
[15] *Glossa interlinearis in 1 Cor.* 6; Aquinas, *Expositio in 1 Cor.* 6.
[16] Gen. 1.16.
[17] Cf. Ps. Dionysius, *Epistola* 9 c.1. Bleienstein suggests Aquinas, *Comm. in I Sent.* d.11 q.1 a.1.
[18] Isidore of Seville, *In Genesim* c.2 PL 83.813.

pretation of the text be granted. Even so, their argument supports our case. For though the moon can only light up the night through illumination it receives from the sun, yet the moon has a virtue proper to itself, given to it by God, which it does not receive from the sun, by which it can cause cold and wet, the very opposite of what the sun causes. Thus each has its own quality, and so in our case: the prince has instruction about the faith from pope and church whilst still having his own proper distinct power which he does not receive from the pope but from God directly without intermediary.

5. Pope Zachary deposed the king of the Franks and put Pepin in his place.[19]

I reply to this argument as follows: the Gloss comments on the word *deposed*, 'that is to say, gave consent to those who were doing the deposing'.[20] History does not say that Zachary deposed the king of the Franks. The *Chronicles* record that Childeric, who was ruling in France, was wholly idle and neglectful of his duties, whilst Pepin, called steward of the household, was in practice sole ruler of the Franks, his brother Charles being a monk. The barons sent from France therefore, to Pope Zachary, asking him to solve the problem for them as to who ought to be king: he who was only nominally king because he had given himself to a life of dissolution or he who was in fact bearing the burden of the government of the kingdom. When the Pope made answer to them that it should rather be he who governed the more usefully, the Franks immediately removed Childeric and his wife to a monastery

[19] *Decretum* C.15 q.6 c.3.
[20] *Glossa ordinaria ad Decretum* C.15 q.6 c.3.

and made Pepin their king, St Boniface, archbishop of Mainz anointing him. This is the account Martin has given in his *Chronicles*.[21] Other narratives tell how after Childeric had reigned for four years, he received the monk's tonsure from piety. Prince Pepin was then appointed king and anointed as such by choice of the barons, and by authority of the pope also in so far as he pronounced on the barons' problem. But the barons could have made him king for some reasonable cause without papal assent.

From all this, it is clear that no pope has ever deposed a king of France, except in the sense explained above by the Gloss, namely that he consented to what was being done by those who were performing the actual deposition. It is inappropriate to draw conclusions from such events which, happening as they do perhaps through devotion to the Church or to a particular person or through good will or some other cause, are of their nature unique, and not indicative of any principle of law. The same histories record that Boniface, sixty-fourth incumbent of the see of Rome, secured from the Emperor Phocas recognition of Rome's primacy of all the churches, because Constantinople had begun to describe itself as firsét before all.[22] If a similar method of argument were used, it would be possible to argue that it was the emperor's business to transfer the primacy of churches or to establish their precedence. Sozomenus wrote in his *Tripartite History* that the Emperor Constantine took part in councils of the

---

[21] Cf. Vincent of Beauvais, *Speculum Historiale* 23.154.
[22] *Speculum historiale* 22.107.

clergy. Rufinus speaks of this in his *Ecclesiastical History* in telling how, when bishops had assembled from almost every part of the world, they began to quarrel among themselves about different matters, the order of business was often interrupted and individuals circulated written accusations. Constantine, seeing that these quarrels were frustrating the settlement of the very important question at issue, fixed a day when any bishop might put forward any complaint he might have. On the appointed day, he seated himself, took up the documents of individual complaint, put them together in his lap and without opening them to examine the contents, addressed the bishops: 'God has made you priests and has given you power to judge us and rightly are we judged by you. You who have been given to us by God as gods, cannot be judged by men, because it is not fitting that man should judge the things of God. Rather should man look for the judgment of God coming from you, as it is written, "God stood in the assembly of the gods etc.". Stop all these present quarrels of yours'. After commanding this, he ordered all the records of the complaints to be burned. Are we to conclude from this evidence that it is the prince's business to intervene in bishops' councils and, in similar fashion, to settle their dissensions and legal disputes? Hugh of Fleury says in Book 5 of his *Chronicle* that Constantine sanctioned and laid down in his will that everything in the ecclesiastical order was to be at the decision and judgment of the bishops of Rome, and in a letter to all the bishops, which Isidore has preserved, the same Emperor Constantine declared: 'We order that the Roman see shall hold primacy over the four major sees, Antioch, Alexandria,

Constantinople and Jerusalem'.[23] In his will which holy
Church preserves so gratefully and which occupies a place
in the *Decretum,*[24] he ordains that the pope holding office
at any time shall take precedence over all the priests of the
world and that it shall be for him to decide what has to
be decided concerning the worship of God and the
stability of the faith of the Christian community. Are we
to conclude then, that because of these dispositions, the
Roman Church has its primacy over the churches and their
administration from the emperors? Certainly not. Again,
we read how at the first Jerusalem council, when the
usage of the old law was in question, the argument flowed
this way and that, until Peter rose to show by arguments
of reason that the yoke of the old law should not be
imposed on the Christian people. It was James, however, who promulgated by pontifical authority the definitive
verdict, because the question had arisen in the church of
Jerusalem whose bishop he was, and could not have been
transferred to another church except on appeal; therefore
James used the expression 'I judge etc.'.[25] Are we then
to say that although the Roman Church is head, it can only
exercise its jurisdiction in cases of appeal from the churches
of other bishops? Certainly not. In the time of the
Emperor Henry, the Romans took an oath not to elect a
pope without the emperor's consent.[26] Is this then to be
observed now? Surely not. I have mentioned these events
to make it clear that legal principles should not be deduced

---

[23] The source for these various historical narratives is the *Speculum Historiale,*
especially Bk. 13.

[24] *Decretum* D.96 c.14.

[25] Acts 15.19.

[26] *Speculum Historiale* 25.27.

from unique events which occurred in particular circumstances.

6. The argument based on Pope Nicholas's statement that Christ has conferred on Peter the rights of both heavenly and earthly empires.[27]

When it is the power of the pope in temporal affairs that is at issue, evidence for the pope from an imperial source carries weight, but evidence for the pope from a papal source does not carry much weight, unless what the pope says is supported by the authority of Scripture. What he says on his own behalf should not be accepted especially when, as in the present case, the emperor manifestly says the contrary and so too do other popes. Pope Nicholas's words may be understood in many different ways. One way has already been mentioned earlier, that is, when for the sake of the common need of the spiritual good, he may order a levy, not only on the property of the clergy, but also on that of the laity.[28] A second way to understand the statement is: the Lord entrusted the rights of both heavenly and earthly kingdoms to Peter, in that he gave him power to absolve and bind on earth so that his sentence, absolution and binding, when the key is not defective, are approved in heaven, as he was told at the commission of the keys: 'Whatsoever thou shalt bind on earth shall be bound also in heaven etc.', just as the Glosses on Matthew 18 explain. The Pope does not seem to have taken his terminology from any source other than the Lord's own words to Peter: 'And to you I will give the keys of the kingdom of heaven' especially since he uses

---

[27] *Decretum* D.22 c.1.
[28] Cf. p. 104 above.

the words, 'to blessed Peter keybearer of the kingdom...' as if alluding to the words with which the power was committed to Peter. Since therefore, the saints do not allow St Peter any power from this text other than the spiritual power, as has been said, as all the exegetes of this text and of Matthew 10 agree, it ought not to be maintained that the Pope meant anything different. There is a third tenable way in which to interpret the Pope's words: Christ did grant the rights of both heavenly and earthly kingdom to the heavenly empire'.[29] Fourthly, there him the spiritual power of uniting the citizens of the earthly kingdom to those of the heavenly. It was in this sense that Maximus spoke of Christ in his Epiphany sermon: 'He is that great king who came to join the earthly kingdo mto the heavenly empire'.[29] Fourthly, there are doctors of canon law who explain the words of Pope Nicholas in this way: 'Christ gave Peter the rights of the heavenly and earthly empires, that is, right to rule heavenly and earthly affairs, that is, to rule clergy and laity who are, so to say, the two walls of the Church, both of which the pope rules in spiritual affairs'.

[29] Maximus Taurinensis, *Homilia de Epiphania Domini* 27 PL 57.285.

CHAPTER XV

Replies to the second set of six arguments

7. The imperial oath to the pope.

The Emperor Otto swore no oath to the pope, except one for the kingdom of Italy which he received as a fief from the pope or the Church. In addition, he swore to return any territories belonging to St Peter, if there were any in his possession. This had nothing to do with other parts of the world which either were not in the empire or did not fall under the donation of Constantine.

8. The pope deposes an emperor.

This is true of anyone whom he has established in office who has received a fief from him, if the cause be a reasonable one. But these arguments are about *de facto* situations, being concerned with what has in fact been done, rather than with what ought to have been done. There are many arguments concerned with past practice which can be used to demonstrate the contrary of this alleged papal power, as was shown above in the refutation of the fifth argument.

9. The pope has translated the Empire.

This proposition can be dealt with in the same way as the preceding proposition. It can be added, however, that Constantine did not make a simple gift of the Empire to the Church. He gave the city of Rome and certain western provinces and the imperial symbols to do with the rulership of these provinces, and then transferred the seat of government with the full dignity of the Empire to Constantinople. To the statement that the pope afterwards translated the Empire from Greeks to Germans, I reply: he did not translate the reality of the Roman Empire but merely the title, because the Romans were annoyed because the Empire, or the name of the Empire, had been transferred from them to Constantinople. They therefore called on Charles to defend them and when he was victorious, acclaimed him, and gave him the title of emperor. From that time, it is as if the Empire had been divided, two emperors being acknowledged. Moreover, this act was not performed by the pope alone, but with the people making acclamation and concession. The people has the right to subject itself to whom it wills without any previous decision of anyone else. This act was accomplished for a necessary and reasonable cause, namely defence of the people against infidels and pagans, when there seemed no possibility of any other defender presenting himself. It was quite legal for the people to do this, for it is the people which makes a king and the army which makes the emperor. Are more arguments needed? This was done by God's special advice for the defence of the Church, as was shown persuasively to the Emperor Constantine I, when the angel appeared to him in the guise of an armed soldier. There is no reason why what has validity in private law, necessarily has validity in public law. All the historical facts mentioned here are recorded in the book *About Cosmography*, Book 5 of Hugh of Fleury's *Chronicles* and the *Chronicles* of Sigibert.[1] Whatever was done in this matter, the Pope ordered nothing except in what had been granted to him by Constantine and here I grant that he could legally make dispositions.

---

[1] Cf. Vincent of Beauvais, *Speculum Historiale* 23.176.

10. The pope can legitimize for civil purposes.

He may so legitimize in his own territory where he has civil jurisdiction, otherwise he may only do so by way of consequence as Johannes [Teutonicus] has pointed out: or better, he cannot even do so by way of consequence in territory not subject to his jurisdiction, and the claim of the decretal that in dispensing in the spiritual order he indirectly dispenses by consequence in the temporal, is to be understood as referring to territory under his jurisdiction, where, when he has both powers, in granting the higher power it is to be understood that the lesser power is granted also. But outside his own territory, he may not legitimize save in the spiritual order, and the *glossa ordinaria* notes this, in the same context.[2] Yet I personally think that in the case of those whose illegitimacy derives from the marriage of parents, forbidden to marry by ecclesiastical law, the pope may dispense them wherever they live and legitimize them in both the spiritual and temporal orders, in that he may legalize the marriage of their parents and make them persons permitted to marry. On the other hand, if the illegitimacy arises because of marriage of those prohibited by natural or divine law then he may not dispense generally and legitimize in the temporal order.

11. The pope on occasion absolves soldiers from their oaths of fidelity.

This is another *de facto* argument. As to its relevance to the French, I reply that it was a declaration of what the law was, namely that in the particular case at issue the oath did not bind, and was not an absolution from an

---

[2] *Decretales* 4.17.13 and *glossa ordinaria*.

oath of fidelity. For this was done with the consent of a king who, perhaps conscious of his unsuitability and wishing to leave public life to devote himself to prayer, chose the monastic life. In such a case the barons could proceed with the election of another king, as had been counselled by the pope, after they had consulted him. It must be borne in mind, however, that a vassal is bound to his natural lord by a double tie: by reason of the property which he accepted under defined terms from his lord with the honour of vassalage, and also by the bond of the oath. The pope cannot absolve from the natural bond; he can pronounce, in a case such as when the prince is a heretic, that a vassal is not bound to follow his lord but should free himself from his obligation and hand back his fief. But he can absolve from the oath of obligation for reasonable and evident cause and in good faith; otherwise absolution from obligation does not hold in God's sight, since power has been given to the pope, as has been said earlier, not to destroy but to build up, as the Apostle says.[3] Whatever about the oath, there always remains that natural obligation which goes with the property, unless the fief is handed back.

12. The pope has cognizance of every crime.

It is clear from what is said in the beginning of c. 13 that this proposition is true when there is doubt concerning sin, that is to say, whether an action is or is not sinful, lawful or unlawful. This is decided according to natural or divine law and is therefore a matter for ecclesiastical decision. But he does not have jurisdiction over

[3] Cf. 2 Cor. 13-10.

sin arising from commerce for this is judged according to human laws. Another explanation is that the pope has jurisdiction of every crime, but in the sphere of conscience, where he is bound to believe the person confessing.

CHAPTER XVI

Replies to the third set of six arguments

13. Concerning denunciation.

The Pope himself answers this argument in the decretal cited.[1] For denunciation does not give the pope jurisdiction. If it did, all civil jurisdiction would be utterly obliterated, since every case could be denounced to the pope by one or other of the parties involved. But as the Pope said in his decretal, his intention was not to judge a feudal matter which was the province of the French king, unless by chance some special privilege existed or some contrary custom whereby the ordinary law might be changed, but to decide a matter of sin. Without any doubt, this was his province, as he said himself, and the proofs he then brought forward were to establish that principle.

14. 'If thy brother shall offend against thee etc. ... tell the Church'.

Chrysostom explains this text: '"To the Church", that is to those who are in charge of the Church'.[2] If, however, 'church' is understood in the general sense, not narrowly as the clerical community but as the community of the faithful, then those in charge of it are the ecclesiastical judge in spiritual matters and the secular in temporal. Or it can be said that reference in the text is to when there is a problem concerning sin. Thus on the text, 'On

---

[1] *Decretales* 2.1.13.
[2] Matth. 18.15, 17 and *glossa ordinaria*.

the lips of two or three etc.', the Gloss has this to say: 'If
he had said there was no sin, so that they should prove sin
had been committed'.[3] Thus if he will not acquiesce, the
Church, which judges sin, must be informed.

15. Concerning Theodosius.

As the jurists note, this law has been abrogated. Innocent gave it weight because the principle in the law is a
live one and knowledge of it is useful in order that it
might be known in what devotion that legislator held the
Church. It was to show this that the law was given a
place in the *Decretum* as 11 q. 1 *Quicunque vitam habens*.[4]
Moreover, we may draw the conclusion that by decree of
princes, an ecclesiastical judge may have cognizance of
such temporal matters. But if such jurisdiction was given
to him by decree of princes, it must not be concluded that
he got it in his capacity as vicar of Christ. It is the
opposite conclusion that can be drawn. It may be said that
princes can, though they ought not, revoke their privileges
and graces and those of their predecessors, just as conversely
popes revoke or can revoke graces they have granted to
princes.

16. The text of Deuteronomy, 'If thou perceive that there
be among you a hard and doubtful matter in judgment etc.'[5]
This is the one special case where it is permissible to have
recourse from a secular to an ecclesiastical judge, namely,
when the secular judge is in doubt, especially when the
doubt is about sin. Another explanation is that recourse is
not so much to the priest as to whoever was judge at the

---

[3] Matth. 18.16 and *glossa ordinaria*.
[4] *Decretum* 11 q.1 c.35.
[5] Deut. 17.8.

time and this is to be understood as a secular judge. So then, there is one judge in spiritual cases and another in temporal. The text says metaphorically: 'To the priests of the Levitical race and to the judge', and this is how the Gloss explains it.[6]

17. The pope has power in the greater, hence in the lesser.

This principle is true when the greater and the lesser are ordered in the same logic; for example, it is true that when a bishop has power to ordain a priest, he has power to ordain a deacon. But it is not true when the orders or genus are different: if my father can generate a man, it does not follow that he can generate a dog nor that if a priest can absolve from sin, he can absolve from a money debt.

18. On the ordering of the temporal to the spiritual.

My answer is clear from what I argued above in chapter seven.

[6] Deut. 17.9 and *glossa ordinaria*.

CHAPTER XVII

Replies to the fourth set of six arguments

19.   Concerning legacies and restitutions.

Legacies for pious purposes fall within the province of ecclesiastical law; this is a spiritual matter, as churchmen say, especially when the legacies are undefined, in which case they can be determined by ecclesiastical law in accordance with whatever wishes the testator may have expressed. Yet I cannot see that it is possible for him to make any valid change in the wish of the testator by way of transference: for example, if the testator bequeathed one hundred pounds to the poor of the city and diocese of Paris, that this could be transferred to the poor of Chartres diocese. But a prince who rules the territory of both dioceses or provinces may effect such a transference should there be a reasonable cause, because he is of the diocese named and not outside it. About restitutions, I cannot see why, through the provision of suitable good men, there should not be allocation to pious purposes for the good of the country, as necessity urges or utility requires, and specially by provision of the prince who watches over the common welfare; when the legatees are unknown he could dispose of the bequests according to the common need and welfare. Because the ecclesiastical judge is permitted to judge the crime of usury because of the sort of crime it is, he has to judge whether restitution ought or ought not to be made. Nevertheless by reason of the forfeiture involved, it pertains to the prince, who is justice personified, and its guardian, to impose the restitution and amendment, and the same holds good in other contracts. It applies even in cases when its applicability seems less obvious. Cognizance of heretics belongs to the ecclesiastical judge, *Extra. De hereticis c. Ad abolendam* and the following *c. Vergentis;*[1] princes negligent in fulfilling their duty are censured and punished by the pope. But this was ordered with the consent of the emperor who was present, as Innocent notes.[2] Then again, it is because the bishop of a city has from the emperor his faculty of supervising the administration of the goods of an estate, and of acting as executor when the testator has not appointed one, that when he has obtained the monies involved, he must notify the rector of the province of the amount involved, and the time when he collected it, as *Code, De sacrosanctis episcopis l. Nulli licere*[3] lays down. Again, civil law enacts in the law, *Digest, De petitione hereditatis l. Hereditas,*[4] which the canonists have taken over,[5] that the defence and execution of last wills as well as other matters pertaining to pious purposes is not a matter for the prelate alone, but belongs principally to the prince: for it states in its concluding section that, 'by the authority of the principal and prelate', that is, of prince and prelate, 'heirs are compelled to comply with the terms of the last will'. Again, a case such as one concerning restitution of debt would seem to belong more to the category of cases of justice rather than cases of piety,

[1] *Decretales* 5.7.9, 10.
[2] *Recte* Lucius III, at whose council of Verona (1184), Emperor Frederick I was present when *Ad abolendam* was promulgated.
[3] *Corpus Iuris Civilis*, Code 1.3.28.
[4] *Id.* Digest 5.3.50.
[5] Cf. *Decretales* 3.26.6 *glossa ordinaria s.v. ab episcopo.*

and therefore I consider that such restitution is not a matter solely for the ecclesiastical judge, but rather is the concern of the prince, though it would be permissible for it to be done perhaps by the disposition of certain good men. **20.** The corporeal is ruled by the spiritual and depends on it causatively.

This argument is fallacious as it is put, on a number of counts. It fails in the first place because it assumes that royal power is corporeal and not spiritual and that its charge is of bodies and not of souls. This is false for, as has been shown above, its purpose is the common good of the citizens; not any good indeterminately, but that good which is to live according to virtue. Hence the Philosopher says in his *Ethics* that the intention of the legislator is to make men good and lead them to virtue[6] and in the *Politics* he says that just as the soul is better than the body, so is the legislator better than the doctor because the legislator has charge of souls, the doctor of bodies.[7] The argument fails in the second place, because it is not any secular power whatsoever which is instituted, moved and directed by any spiritual power whatsoever. In a well-ordered household it is not he who teaches letters and morals, a spiritual function, who appoints the physician; both are appointed by the head of the household. Nor does he direct the physician in his medical capacity, but only incidentally in so far as the physician might wish to be chaste or liberally educated. So then it is not the pope who appoints a king; each is appointed by God to his own proper sphere. Nor does the pope direct a king in his royal capacity, but incidentally,

---

[6] *Nic. Ethics* 2.1.
[7] Bleienstein suggests *Pol.* 7.2 and possibly 4.4.

in so far as a king is concerned to be a faithful christian; the pope directs him in faith but not in government. Thus he is subject to the pope in those things in which the supreme power has made him subject, namely spiritual matters only. The argument then, is obviously false; indeed were we to consider examples, it would rather support our view than contradict it. Heavenly bodies are moved towards their end and administered by angels, yet they were not made by angels, but by God without intermediary. The conclusion must be drawn then, that earthly power is from God without intermediary, although it is directed by the spiritual power to a life of beatitude.

21. The opinion of Hugh of St Victor that the spiritual power appoints the temporal.[8]

To this it can be said that Hugh's words are not authoritative and carry little weight. It can be said, as Augustine does in the *On diverse questions,* that it is the usage of sacred scripture to say that something has happened when it is made manifest.[9] It was in this sense that Hugh was saying that the pope established the royal power; not indeed by bringing it into existence, since it comes from God and from the choice and assent of the people, but by making manifest the institution and choice of a king in anointing him.

22. 'But the spiritual man judgeth all things: and he himself is judged of no man'.[10]

It is assumed, often and in different contexts, that this

---

[8] Cf. Hugh of St Victor, *De sacramentis* 2.2.4.

[9] Accepting here Bleienstein's correction of Leclercq's attribution of the citation to *De civitate Dei*. The reference is, *De diversis quaestionibus* 1.69.4 PL 40.75-6.

[10] 1 Cor. 2.15.

text refers to the authority of the pope. Yet this is not what it says. The 'spiritual man' referred to is not spiritual because he holds the spiritual power which an ecclesiastical judge holds, for sometimes he who holds such power may be a man who is 'sensual' in the sense of the word used in this text. A man may be described as sensual according to his way of life or according to his manner of thinking. He is said to be sensual in his way of life if it is characterized by licentiousness unrestrained by the guidance of the spirit; in his manner of thinking, should he decide about God on the evidence of physical bodies or the letter of the law or by the principles of physics. A man may be described as spiritual according to his way of life or according to his knowledge. His way of life is spiritual if, possessing the spirit of God, he rules his life by the guidance of that spirit; he is spiritual in knowledge when decisions about God are not made according to human ways of thought but are formed in certainty and fidelity through faith, in subjection to the Holy Spirit. Hence the text should be read: it is the man who is spiritual in the sense explained 'who judgeth all things', Gloss: 'hidden things by sure faith'; 'and he himself is judged of no one', Gloss: 'that is, it is understood whether he understand well or ill' or 'judged by no one', that is, 'is reproved by no one'. This is how Jerome and Augustine explain the text[11] and the letter of the Apostle which follows bears out what they say.

23.   Concerning the order of ends.

This argument too is defective in many ways. Firstly, because the art to which the higher end pertains does not

---

[11] *Glossa ordinaria ad 1 Cor.* 2.15.

move and control the art to which the lower end pertains in any absolute sense, but only relatively to the need of its own final end; this explanation to some extent is conceded in the proposition. Further, it is defective because the higher art does not always and necessarily control the movement of the lower by way of authority or by establishing it, but commands it solely by way of guidance. For example, the physician instructs the pharmacist and judges whether or not the medicines have been properly compounded. But he has no power to appoint or discharge him. For there is a superior over both physician and pharmacist on whom rests the whole order of the community, namely its king or lord. It is for him to appoint the pharmacist and to remove him if he fails to fulfil the physician's requirements. In the same way, the whole world is a single community under God as its supreme power who appoints etc., both pope and prince. There is a third way in which the argument is defective. It has some point where what constitutes the lower art does not have anything good or desirable in itself, but is ordered only for the higher end towards which the higher art looks, just as mixing of medicines, the work of the pharmacist, is for the sake of health, which is the end at which the physician aims. But it has no validity where what is of the lower art is good and desirable in itself; into this category falls living according to virtue. For many things are good and desirable in themselves and yet are ordered to something else, as the Philosopher says about friendship in Book 8 of his *Ethics* and about knowing and seeing and such like, in Book 10.[12] The fourth reason why the

[12] *Nic. Ethics* 8.1; 10.3.

argument is fallacious is this. Let it be conceded that it would be valid in certain ordered particulars, where the lower end leads to a higher end in one fixed way, and where to fail in that way constitutes an unqualified failure, with the lower end remaining inoperative in relation to the higher end. Yet where the lower end is related to the higher in different ways, it does not follow of necessity that if it fails in one relationship the power established in it becomes quite useless, since it is related to the end in another way — a way which is perhaps known only to the supreme power and for the sake of which he wishes the lower power to remain useful. So it is then with royal power. Through this power, the people are directed to God, not only when the king uses his power as king but also when he uses it as a tyrant; tyranny of princes can exist for punishment of sinners, for as Job says, God makes a man that is a hypocrite to reign for the sins of the people,[13] or to prove the endurance of subjects, or to force them to take refuge with God who alone can change the hearts of kings for the better; as Solomon says, 'The heart of the king is in the hand of the Lord: whithersoever he will he shall turn it'.[14] God can even deprive tyrants of their power if he considers them unworthy of a change of heart, as is said in the Book of Wisdom: 'God hath over-turned the thrones of proud princes: and hath set up the meek in their stead'.[15] And through Ezechiel he says: 'I will deliver my flock from their mouth and it shall no more be meat for them'.[16]

[13] Cf. Job 34.30.
[14] Prov. 21.1.
[15] Eccles. 10.17.
[16] Ezech. 34.10.

24. It is for the pope to give laws to princes and a prince cannot make laws, nor use them, until they have been approved by the pope.

That this is false is expressly stated by Pope Leo writing to the emperor Lotharius, D.10 *c. De capitulis*:[17] 'Concerning your imperial chapters and decrees and those of your predecessors, we avow that we have been able and are able under Christ's favour, to guard and conserve them inviolate, and will preserve them now and for ever in every way. And if anyone has told you, or shall tell you otherwise, account him certainly a liar'. Civil laws are not altered by the canons except in spiritual cases; the pope cannot change the laws except for the practice of his own court, as Johannes Teutonicus[18] and others say. But to say, as these other masters are saying, that the pope gives laws to princes and that princes cannot take laws from any other source unless they have been approved by the pope, is to destroy royal and political governance altogether, and to fall into the error of Herod who thought fearfully that Christ would destroy the earthly kingdom. For according to what the Philosopher writes in Book 1 of the *Politics,* a constitution is described as royal only when whoever rules does so according to laws he has himself made. When, however, he rules not according to his own will but according to laws which the citizens and others have made, this is said to be a civil or political constitution, not a monarchical one.[19] If then no prince were to rule except

---

[17] *Decretum* D.10 c.9.

[18] *Glossa ordinaria ad Decretum* D.10 c.4 *s.v. Constitutiones.*

[19] John of Paris possibly had in mind here Aquinas, *In libros Politicorum expositio* n. 13 (ad *Pol.* 1.1.3, 4).

by laws given by the pope, or first approved by him, no one would be governed by either royal or a political government, but only by papal rule, which is to destroy the kingdom and to make void every long-established government.

CHAPTER XVIII

Replies to the fifth set of six arguments

25. The priesthood is called royal because priests are kings.

It is clear from what I have said already that the priest-hood is called royal not in relation to the kingdom of the world, but in relation to the kingdom of heaven, towards which it orders and guides the faithful. Or again: according to the mind of St Peter,[1] this is said to all faithful and just men who, in constituting a unity with Christ their head, are kings and priests in him: 'the attribution to the members of what belongs to the head' according to the rule of Tichonius.[2] Or again: they are called a kingdom, because Christ their king rules in them, and called priests, because they offer to God the sacrifice of praise and an afflicted spirit.[3] This, indeed, is what all just men offer.

26. Concerning the Old Testament anointing of a king by a priest.

It is not a necessity of the nature of secular power that it should be anointed, since before there were anointed kings in the Jewish people, there were such leaders as Moses and Joshua and their successors, from whom the Lord made provision for government. Nor is it a necessity of kingship itself, the authority of which is more complete than that of those leaders, that a king be anointed, since other nations have kings who are not anointed. But in the

[1] 1 Peter 2.9.
[2] Tichonius, *Liber de septem regulis* 1 PL 18.15-16.
[3] Cf. Ps. 50.19.

Jewish people, kings were anointed as the mystery and prefiguration of Christ the king who was to be born of that people, who was 'anointed with the oil of grace and gladness above thy fellows':[4] 'with the oil', namely, the oil prefigured by the oil with which the kings of that people were anointed. This too is observed amongst Christian kings who by being anointed, make acknowledgment of their membership of Christ. For it is not inappropriate for kings of the people of God to be true kings and also figurations of the high king: as Augustine says: 'The performance of this royal anointing by the priest was commanded as a sign that there would be born in that people he who would be both king and priest, namely Christ'.[5] But since many of the institutions of the Jewish people were figurative, they are not to be given a place in the Christian people. We do not read in the New Testament that priests should anoint kings, nor is the practice of anointing observed by all Christian kings. The kings of Spain, for example, do not. The argument, therefore, adds nothing to the proposition. Further, Old Testament anointing was consecration, and according to Papias, to consecrate is to give to God. It follows, then, that no conclusion can be drawn about the superiority of the priesthood over the royal power in temporal matters and affairs of the world, but only in the affairs of God. Similarly, that the sins of kings are expiated by the offerings of priests does not prove the priesthood to be greater than the royal power, except in the one context of what belongs

---

[4] Heb. 1.9.
[5] Cf. *Enarratio in Ps. XLIV*. This is not a direct quotation. It is possibly a précis of Augustine on Ps. 44.9.

to God, as is said in 2 q. 7 *c. Nos si incompetenter*.[6] A further demonstration of the inconclusiveness of the argument lies in the fact that those priests of the old law who anointed kings were indubitably subject to those kings.

27.   Society cannot be ruled without justice.

It must be said that acquired moral virtues can be complete without theological virtues; they are not completed by them, except by a certain incidental completion, as Augustine suggested in the book of his opinions compiled by Prosper.[7] Thus there is that true and complete justice necessary to the government of a kingdom without Christ's rulership, since a kingdom is ordered to life according to acquired moral virtue. This may be completed incidentally by virtues of other sorts. Or it can be put this way: Augustine's argument was that there is no true justice where Christ is not ruler, not because it could not exist at all, but because there was not even acquired virtue in a society whose members were in slavery to demons and idols and yet believed they served justice. It was these people whom Augustine denounced as not preserving true justice. It can be said that the commonwealth of the Christian people is not rightly ruled unless its leader is the pope who is the vicar of Christ in spiritual things, nor can justice be preserved otherwise than by obedience to him, as is just, in spiritual matters.

28.   It is fitting that powers 'ordained of God'[8] should be related in a particular way (namely, with the secular

---

[6]   *Decretum* C.2 q.7 c.41.
[7]   St Augustine does not say this in Prosper of Aquitaine's *Liber Sententiarum ex operibus s. Augustini deliberatarum*.
[8]   Rom. 13.1.

power mediated through the spiritual power, not taking its origin from God directly).

As has been said already, the powers are related in an order of dignity, not of causality; the one does not have its origin in the other. The parallel is with the hierarchy of angels. All angels were created by God in such an order of dignity that it is natural for the one always to be more noble than another, without, however, establishing an order of causality whereby the one has its origin from the other. All were created by God without any intermediate agent. The intention of the Apostle seems to be to speak of the relationship of each power to its own proper end, not of the relationship of one to the other. This is clear from what he has to say of the prince: 'he is God's minister; an avenger, etc.'.[9]

29. Concerning the one head of the Church.

In reply to this argument, it can be said that there is one Church, one Christian people, one mystical body; not indeed in Peter or Linus but in Christ, who alone is the exclusive, supreme head of the Church and from whom came the ordering of the powers each separate from the other, in the diversity of its own ranks. As Ephesians 2 says: 'He has subjected all things under his feet and hath made him head over all the Church, which is his body'; on this text, Ambrose comments: 'He is head according to his humanity'[10] and in chapter 5 it is written: 'Christ is head of the Church'.[11]

Nevertheless the pope can be described also as head of

---

[9] Rom. 13.4.
[10] Ephes. 2.22-23 and *glossa ordinaria*.
[11] Ephes. 5.23.

the Church as to the hierarchy of ministers, in that he is chief minister, from whom, as from the principal vicar of Christ in spiritual matters, the whole order of ministers depends, as from its summit and its foundation, inasmuch as the Roman Church is unquestionable head of all the churches. The pope is not head, however, as to governance of temporal affairs or the management of temporal property. In these respects, each king is head in his own kingdom, and the emperor, if there is one, is monarch and head of the world.

We must here consider a conclusion that some would draw from the existence of an ecclesiastical hierarchy and its need for a supreme single ruler, the pope. They argue that because of that hierarchy, kings and princes are subject to the pope in temporal matters, because both spiritual and temporal powers inhere in the pope; an argument they pursue at great length. But the truth to be learnt from the existence of this ecclesiastical hierarchy is the contrary of this view. According to St Denis, on the lowest grade of the ecclesiastical hierarchy stand laymen with their kings, imperfect men, though capable of perfection; above them are the perfect and above them, in turn, are the more perfect, the clergy, and at the summit, the supreme monarch of all, the pope. It is agreed that according to the teaching of the same Denis the lowest are not connected to the highest except through intermediaries.[12]

Therefore the pope has no general or direct power over the laity except in the same way as the intermediaries have it, in their more restricted way within the hierarchy, as do

[12] Cf. Pseudo-Dionysius, *De ecclesiastica hierarchia* c.5 PG 3.499.

bishops and abbots. Although in the hierarchy of angels the
supreme monarch, who is God, can act in relation to the
lowest of the angels in ways which none of the intermediaries can act, such as creating or reducing to nothing, yet he
does not have this power as God, supreme hierarch, but as
God, creator.[13] Since those who hold the view we are
attacking do not posit that the more perfect intermediaries
have both spiritual and lay powers over the laity but
spiritual power only, it is clear from the structure of the
ecclesiastical hierarchy that the pope in his capacity as
supreme hierarch shall not enjoy any but spiritual power,
although that is more general because it is operative everywhere. In this same context of the ecclesiastical hierarchy,
Bernard, in Book 3 of his *To Pope Eugenius,* attributed no
power to the pope which inferior prelates do not have,
though he attributes supreme power to the pope. Hence he
says: 'You are mistaken if you consider that your apostolic
power is not only the supreme power, but even the only
power instituted by God. If you think this, your opinion
differs from that of the Apostle who says, "There is no
power but from God". Accordingly, that which follows,
"He that resisteth the power, resisteth the ordinance of
God", though applicable chiefly to you, does not apply
exclusively to you. He says as much: "Let every soul be
subject to the higher powers". For he does not say "to
the higher power" as if all was in one man, but "to the
higher powers" as if power resided in many. Your power,
then, is not the only power from the Lord; there are middle
and lower powers'.[14] Here it is made perfectly obvious that

---

13 Meaning that as creator he is outside the hierarchy.
14 St Bernard, *De consideratione* 3.4.

God gives no power to the pope which he does not give to intermediary prelates, though in the pope he has placed the highest power. The conclusion is clear. Since these intermediary prelates have no power from Christ save only spiritual power, the pope alone cannot have temporal power by virtue of his authority as head of the ecclesiastical hierarchy. The saints say this. The very words used in Matthew 16 show that Christ did not give any power to Peter which he did not give to the other apostles and bishops and priests, although Peter is said to have accepted the keys in a special way because of the headship conferred on him by Christ, as Rabanus[15] and the Gloss[16] state. What was said in Matthew 16 to Peter alone was said also in the very same words to all of them, Matthew 18, 'Whatsoever you shall bind etc.'[17]; and similarly the commission recounted in John 20 was to all of them: 'Receive ye the Holy Spirit; whose sins you shall forgive etc.',[18] on which text Chrysostom comments that no more than spiritual power was granted them.[19] I have made this digression because of the opinion of certain eminent people who strive to prove from the unity of the ecclesiastical hierarchy that the pope has both swords. It is worthy of reflexion, however, that in the context of hierarchical order, Bernard rebuked the pope, in the place cited earlier, for upsetting that order when he granted exemptions to abbots and those inferior to bishops, subjecting them directly to his own jurisdiction. There is nothing comparable to this

[15] Rabanus Maurus, *Comm. in Matthaeum* 1.5.
[16] *Glossa ordinaria in Matthaeum* 16.
[17] Matth. 18.18.
[18] John 20.22-23.
[19] *Glossa ordinaria in Matthaeum* 16.

in the celestial hierarchy which provides the exemplar of the ecclesiastical hierarchy. He seems to think that it cannot be done legally, on the grounds that the Lord instructed the pope, prefigured in Moses: 'Look and make it according to the pattern that was shown thee on the mount'.[20] For this intimates dispensation not destruction, since the pope was entrusted with dispensation not destruction. But I do not wholly agree with Bernard's opinion on this point.

30.   Concerning the two swords of the text, 'Lo, here are two swords etc.'.[21]

There is nothing here except a certain allegorical reading from which no convincing argument can be drawn. This is because, as has been said already, according to Denis, mystical theology is not conclusive[22] and, according to Augustine in his *Letter to Vincentius*,[23] allegory is insufficient to prove any proposition unless some clear authority can be produced from another source to substantiate it. I can go further and say that the two swords of this text are not to be understood as referring in the mystical sense to the two powers, especially as none of the saints whose teaching is approved and confirmed by the Church explains the text according to that particular mystical interpretation. Reading the two swords in the mystical sense, they understand it as the word of God, in the meaning of the Apostle's Ephesians 6: 'Take unto you the helmet of salvation and the sword of the spirit, which is the word of God'.[24] Reference, then, is to two

---

[20] Exodus 25.40.
[21] Luke 22.38.
[22] Cf. Pseudo-Dionysius, *Ep*. 9 PG 3.1103 and Aquinas, *Comm. I. Sent.* 11 q.1 a.1.
[23] Cf. Augustine, *Ep*. 93 c.8 PL 33.334.
[24] Ephes. 6.17.

swords symbolizing the old and new testaments. Or again: the two swords refer to the sword of the word and the sword of impending persecution of which Luke spoke concerning blessed Mary: 'Thy own soul a sword shall pierce'[25] and 2 Kings 12: 'The sword shall never depart from thy house'.[26] And these swords ought to be enough: one was the Apostles' in a passive sense, because they would have to bear it, namely, the sword of persecution, and the other specially for themselves to be unsheathed in due season, namely, the sword of the word of God. Let it be granted, however, that the swords the Apostles had should be understood as signifying the spiritual and temporal powers. The text says that two swords are actually there, but it does not say they are to be Peter's or any other Apostle's, for Peter did not touch one of them, namely the secular sword since it was not his. He did touch the other one, namely the spiritual sword which was the only one the Lord says was his, and yet he was not to unsheathe it immediately. Hence he was told: 'Put up thy sword into the scabbard',[27] for certainly an ecclesiastical judge ought not to use his spiritual sword precipitately for fear it might be despised, but only after much consideration and in circumstances of great necessity. Given, then, that the mystical meaning of the two swords is the two powers, the reading supports our position because, although there were two, Peter was given only one for himself. It was for this reason that the Lord also said in Matthew 10: 'I come not to send peace, but the sword',[28] where he says expressly

25 Luke 2.35.
26 Kings 12.10.
27 John 18.11.
28 Matth. 10.34.

'sword' not 'swords' and again, it is said in the Psalms, as if by Christ: 'Gird thy sword upon thy thigh'[29] and Apocalypse 1, in the text about the son of man in the midst of the candlesticks and chapter 19 of him who is called the word of God, it is written, 'out of his mouth proceedeth a sharp two-edged sword'.[30] See then how it is demonstrated that he has but the one sword from Christ. This can be said, nevertheless. Two swords were said to have been there and to belong to the Apostles in this sense: one is theirs' and their successors' in itself, given to them by Christ: the other is authorized to be theirs' as occasion warrants because it is not incompatible with their calling and was going to be theirs' in the future, given to them by the grant and permission of princes. It can also be claimed that the authority of Bernard is on our side because he says: 'Both swords belong to the Church, but the material sword ought to be used on be-half of the Church, the spiritual sword by the Church; the one is wielded by the priest, the other by the soldier, but of course at the request of the priest and the command of the emperor'.[31] Bernard says expressly, 'at the request of the priest and the command of the emperor' and not 'by his own hand or at his command', because here he has no authority to command or compel, but only to intimate. Command is only if the emperor wishes it.

[29] Ps. 44.4.
[30] Apoc. 1.13, 16; 19.13, 15.
[31] *De consideratione* 4.3.

CHAPTER XIX

Replies to the sixth set of six arguments

31. The argument put forward by Henry of Cremona.

Although this writer boasts that much of what he had to say was free of doubt, what he in fact says is so crude as scarcely to merit repetition. Nevertheless let us run through his arguments one by one. His first claim is that the Lord governed the world by personal rule from its beginning down to the time of the Flood and after that, by rule of his priests, Noah, Abraham, Moses and others. I say that this argument is defective in numerous ways. In the first place, he supposes that these men were priests. In the case of Noah, however, this is manifestly wrong; he was no priest nor is it related of him that he ever performed any of the functions of a priest. It is not an objection here to recall the text about his building an altar to the Lord,[1] because to build an altar or to pray and call on the Lord are not in themselves priestly functions for, on the authority of James 5, they are not special to priests: 'Pray one for another, that you may be saved'.[2] Even if Noah had been a priest, one could not draw the conclusion that God will have ruled the world through a priest, since one does not read that Noah built an altar to God until after he had built and commanded the ark. About Abraham and Moses, it is agreed that they were not truly priests. There

---

[1] Cf. Gen. 8.20.
[2] James 5.16.

was no authentic sacrifice offered before the true sacrifice
of Christ, the first real priest, as was explained earlier in
chapter 4. Nor were they even priests of the law, figurative
of priests, with the dignity and function of such, as Aaron
was, since they were never anointed. Sacrifices had not
then been instituted, though at need and because of the
lack of priests these men performed some of the actions of
priests; for example, Moses anointed Aaron. It is because
of this or some similar action that the Psalmist can speak
of 'Moses and Aaron among his priests etc.';[3] this is the
explanation given by Pope Anacletus in his second letter
to the bishops of Italy.[4] That Abraham is called 'presbyter'
is not relevant to the proposition since, as is said in the
last canon of D.94,[5] a man is called a 'presbyter' because
he is senior not only in age but also in wisdom.

Secondly, even conceding that they were priests, the
argument still fails. For God established them as princes
and it was as princes, not as priests, that they ruled the
people in temporal affairs. Nor does it follow that if the
two powers at that time were not clearly separated as
to the subject of their operation, they ought now to be
combined in one person, because at that time the priesthood was not complete. The more the priesthood developed
towards completion, the sharper its distinction from the
secular power the Lord wished it to become. Hence in
times that knew kings and judges, there were two powers,
separate in their subject. Therefore they ought to be more
so now, as was stated above in chapter 10.

[3] Ps. 98.6.
[4] *Decretum* D.84 c.4.
[5] Recte *Decretum* D.84 c.4, the same text as already cited.

32. Concerning rule over the end and over the means by which the end is attained.

This is an obviously ill-constructed argument. For it is as if to argue along these lines: that man is master of all horses; he is master, therefore, of all bridles. This does not follow, as is obvious to anyone. Also, the argument errs in its factual content, since it is untrue that the pope is lord of the spiritual because he alone is minister, for he is not, as 1 Corinthians 4 says: 'This is how one should regard us, as servants of Christ and stewards of the mysteries of God'.[6] Because there is one Lord of both the spiritual and the temporal, it does not follow that there is but one minister of them. There will be many, as 1 Corinthians 12 says: 'There are diversities of ministries, but the same Lord. And there are diversities of operations, but the same God, who worketh all in all'.[7] Further, the replies given above to the argument concerning ends can be applied to this argument also. Again, Henry of Cremona's additional remark about God giving everything to Peter is silly. For he did not entrust all souls to him so that he should be lord of everyone but in order that he might be their teacher and protector against spiritual wolves. As Bernard told Eugenius: 'You will vanquish the wolves but still not lord it over the sheep'[8] and as Peter says: 'Neither lording it over the clergy but being made a pattern of the flock from the heart'.[9] His argument from the Apostle's words, 'All things are yours',[10] is irrelevant,

[6] 1 Cor. 4.1.
[7] 1 Cor. 12.5-6.
[8] *De consideratione* 2.6.
[9] 1 Peter 5.3.
[10] 1 Cor. 3.22.

because St Paul is not here specifically addressing Peter or the pope, but all the faithful, particularly the just, to whom belong all things for profit and service in attaining the good, in the way in which all things belong to just men, as 23 q.7.[11] Or again, let the text be understood by way of what the Gloss on 1 Corinthians 13, 'Charity seeketh not her own' has to say: 'Charity makes everything common since what an individual does not have in himself, he has in another, with whom he is one in charity'.[12]

33. Because of the sins of emperors, the right of empire has been transferred to the pope.

This is a quite ridiculous argument for five reasons. Firstly, because it is not by divine law that emperors are deprived of rule because of their sins. For as Augustine has shown in his *City of God* Book 4,[13] it is God's will that kingdoms and empires be shared by both the good and the bad alike; it is happiness which he reserves for the good alone. So it is not by divine law that emperors may be deprived of their right to rule because of their sins. Secondly, because not all emperors have committed these crimes nor should their sins be prejudicial to other emperors. This applies especially in relation to the empire, where succession is not hereditary, where formal choice of emperor is by the army and people. Thirdly, because whereas some popes have been found to be wicked and heretical and have been justly deposed, their wickedness has not prejudiced their successors who have been canonically elected. Fourthly, because given that an emperor be deprived of his right

---

[11] *Decretum* 23. q.7 c.1.
[12] 1 Cor. 13.5 and *glossa ordinaria*.
[13] Cf. *De civitate Dei* 4.33 (CSEL 40.5.1.206).

through some fault of his, no right of empire accrues to the pope as a result of that fault. For as St. Augustine says, by sinning a man is justly subject to the devil, but the devil is not acting justly in bearing sway over him.[14] This is particularly relevant to the proposition, because domination is forbidden to the clergy, as was made clear earlier. Fifthly, because the insinuation at the end of the argument that allegiance to emperors derives from a privilege, is false. For no such privilege given to emperors by churchmen has ever been heard of. Rulership is theirs' by law, when the people or army create them, as D.93 c. Legimus,[15] through the inspiration of God, because their power is from God, as 23 q.4 c. Quesitum,[16] while the Commentator on Ethics Book 8 says that a king comes into being by the will of the people, but when he is king it is natural he should have domination.[17]

34. Concerning the greater power the Church has now than at the time of its beginning, and the supporting authorities cited.

As the argument depends on allegory, it is obvious that it is invalid because as Augustine says in the Letter to Vincentius, allegory without clear authority to support it does not suffice for proof and Denis says that mystical theology is not conclusive.[18] Furthermore, concerning the interpretation of Luke 14 on the parable of the supper[19] and the Psalm, 'Why have the Gentiles raged etc.',[20] these

---

[14] Cf. De libero arbitrio 3.10.
[15] Decretum D.93 c.24.
[16] Decretum 23 q.4 c.45.
[17] Cf. Averroes, Moralium Nicomachiorum Paraphrasis 8.7.
[18] These references are given above, p. 196.
[19] Luke 14.16-24.
[20] Ps. 2.1.

texts should rather be read in the moral sense than in the way these people interpret them. The sense concerns the persecution of Christ sustained at present in his members through evil-doers, and his rulership in his members in the future, when, in the Apostle's words, Hebrews 2, all things shall be subject to him in heaven.[21] If, however, 'all things' is interpreted, as they do interpret it, in terms of the state of the Church militant at different times, the interpretation does not establish their position. For as Augustine says in his *Concerning the Lord's Words*,[22] the Lord is not speaking as if the Church can now force Jews and Gentiles to accept the faith, nor is he saying that the Church is not now legally subject in temporal affairs to kings and princes, as it was formerly. He is talking about heretics, for it is to these that the word 'hedges' of the text[23] refers; those who construct hedges cause divisions. Heretics may be lawfully compelled by the Church to return, but the Church did not do this in the beginning because of the limitations of its power, for then princes and kings were not so well-disposed to the Church as they are now, when through the power of princes, heretics can be so compelled. This is how the matter is treated in *Decretum* 23 q.4 and q.6.

35. Concerning the permission to establish a king and God's displeasure.

The argument is fallacious in numerous ways. The Lord appointed a king for the Jewish people at the same time as the priesthood or even before, though admittedly not

---

[21] Hebrews 2.8.
[22] Cf. *Sermo* 102 c.7 PL 38.647.
[23] Luke 14.23.

with fulness of power, as is clear from Moses, Joshua and their successors who ruled over the whole people. Hence Moses used to say, Numbers 27: 'May the Lord, the God of the spirits of all flesh, provide a man, that may be over this multitude'.[24] It is written about the individual judges who followed Joshua, that the Lord raised them up a saviour and that the spirit of the Lord was in them, as appears from Judges 3.[25] These rulers were, then, established by God, not placed in office by decision of the children of Israel. They were a type of king in that each singly ruled over the whole people, itself a type of kingdom. This was not, however, a pure royal constitution, in that it was mixed with aristocracy, in which the many rule according to virtue. It was mixed too with democracy, that is, with rule by the people, as will be seen. When afterwards, at their petition, God allowed them to have a king with fulness of power, he still did not entrust them with the choice, as the argument we are considering alleges. He reserved it to himself, as appears from Deuteronomy 17 where it is said: 'Thou shalt set him whom the Lord thy God shall choose'.[26] It is not derogatory of royal dignity that the concession of a king at their petition was seemingly in displeasure, as 1 Kings 8 suggests.[27] For a similar argument can be urged about a priest, because when Moses said to the Lord, Exodus 4: 'I beseech thee, Lord, send whom thou wilt send. The Lord being angry at Moses said: Aaron the Levite is thy brother. I know

[24] Num. 27.16.
[25] Judges 3.9-10.
[26] Deut. 17.15.
[27] 1 Kings 8.18.

that he is eloquent: he cometh forth to meet thee etc.'.[28] Why did God give them a king when he was angry? The answer must be that it was not because a regal constitution displeased him as being intrinsically evil. God had chosen that people as peculiarly his own, as Deuteronomy 7 makes clear,[29] and had at first instituted for them a better constitution than a pure royal one, namely one of mixed type. This was better, at least for that people, for two reasons.

Firstly, although a constitution in which one single individual rules according to virtue is better than any other form of single rule, as the Philosopher shows in Book 3 of his *Politics*,[30] nonetheless, joined with aristocracy and democracy, it is better than the pure form, because, in a mixed constitution, all have some share in government. For through this sharing, the peace of the community is preserved, everybody loves a government of this type and watches over it, as is said in *Politics* Book 2.[31] Such was the constitution best instituted by God in that people: it was royal, in that one single person ruled over all, as did Moses and Joshua; it had also something of aristocracy about it, which is leadership by some of the best people according to virtue, because under the one ruler seventy-two elders were chosen, as Deuteronomy 1;[32] there was, too, something of democracy, the rule of the people, because the seventy-two were chosen from and by all the people, as is said in the same place. Thus it was the best

---

[28] Exodus 4.13-14.
[29] Deut.7.6.
[30] Cf. *Pol.* 3.11-12.
[31] Cf. *ibid.* 2.9; 4.7-12.
[32] This is not an accurate account of what Deut. 1 says.

mixture because everyone had a place and a share in the constitution. It would certainly be the best constitution for the Church if, under the one pope, many were chosen by and from each province, so that all would participate in some way in the government of the Church.

There was a second reason why such a constitution was better for that people than an unmixed royal constitution. A regal constitution is best in itself if it is not corrupt. Nevertheless because of the magnitude of the power granted to a king, a kingdom easily degenerates into a tyranny, unless the man who is given power has perfect virtue. As is stated in Book 10 of the *Ethics,* it is the mark of a virtuous man to carry good fortune well.[33] But perfect virtue is to be found in few, particularly of that people, for the Jews were cruel and given to avarice, the very vices with which tyranny operates. From the beginning, then, the Lord did not appoint a king with such fulness of power, but a judge and director for their protection, on the pattern already described, because this was better suited to them. If then, afterwards, when at their request he appointed a king, he did so as if in displeasure, this was because they were rejecting a constitution more beneficial to them.

The addition to the same argument concerning what was said of kings in Osea 8: 'They have reigned and not by me'[34] is irrelevant, because the text has reference to kings who are wicked. One could say the same about wicked prelates of the Church who do not enter the sheepfold by the door[35] or who abuse the authority they have been

[33] Cf. *Nic. Ethics* 10.6-8.
[34] Osea 8.4.
[35] Cf. John 10.1.

given. Moreover, it can be argued that the authority in question supports our position. Bernard explains it in Book 2 of his *To Pope Eugenius* with reference to popes and prelates who seek lordship. His explanation reads: 'It is clear that lordship is forbidden to the apostles. So you are daring to usurp for yourselves either lordship in virtue of apostleship or apostleship in virtue of lordship. You are clearly debarred from both. Beware of thinking you are excluded from those of whom the Lord complains when he said: "They have reigned, but not by me: they have been princes, and I knew it not"'.[36]

36. The argument concerning the priests' land which under Pharaoh was free of tribute and tax.

It must be said of this authority that it proves priests should be free of burdens which are laid on their persons, their residences or homesteads and on what has been given them for the salvation of souls in their capacity as priests and ministers of God. It does not apply to what churches acquire in commerce or other ways; such property comes to them with its fiscal burden, as is noted in 23 q.8 *c. Tributum* and *c. Secundum canonicam*.[37] The exemption is conceded to churches by princes and emperors, as is stated in these canons.

---

[36] *De consideratione* 2.6.
[37] *Decretum* 23 q.8 c.22, 24.

CHAPTER XX

Replies to the seventh set of six arguments

37. Concerning bishops who when summoned by the pope, on the emperor's command remain at home and are censured for this by the pope.

It is to be noted that the canon cited concerns only those bishops who are content with the Levitical portion only, as Johannes Teutonicus noted when glossing that text[1] and also *c. Quo ausu* of the same *quaestio*. It is not intended to cover the case of those bishops who hold rights of the king or possessions of other sorts; such come to them still bearing the appropriate commitments. These bishops are bound to obey their lords just like everybody else. The canon following expressly makes this distinction[2]. Attention should be paid to what seems a very comparable case: a monk who becomes a bishop is more subject to his archbishop than to his abbot and owes him prior obedience. Likewise a monk translated to a parish cure owes greater obedience to the local bishop in what concerns his parochial charge than to his abbot and the bishop can make visitation and correct him. Thus a bishop who accepts feudalities, especially when the pope knows and allows him to do so, owes prior allegiance to his temporal lord than to the pope, and in a case where the prince has issued him some command touching his feudal obligations, it would seem that

---

[1] *Decretum* 23 q.8 c.18; and *glossa ordinaria s.v. orationibus.*
[2] *Ibid.* c.26; *glossa ordinaria s.v. nullum omnino.*

he is exempt from obedience to the pope in the same way as is the monk from his abbot. That is how Hugh of St Victor decides the matter in his *On the Sacraments* part 2, chapter 4, when he says that princes who endow the church cannot make a total transfer of lordship to a degree where they retain no right as lord at all. This is his statement of the matter: 'The Church can have lay persons as stewards through whom it can carry into effect laws and judgments relating to matters concerning the lay power according to the tenor of the civil laws and obligation under human law, provided that the stewards acknowledge that the power they have is from a lay prince and appreciate that these possessions can never be withdrawn from royal power. For if, when reason and necessity demand, the lay power is bound to protect the property of the Church, then likewise in times of need, those same possessions should be at the service of the civil power. For just as royal power cannot hand over to another its duty of giving protection, so when churchmen hold possessions, they cannot lawfully reject the allegiance owed to the royal power in return for its protection: as it is written, "Render to Caesar the things that are Caesar's: and to God the things that are God's"'.[3]

Perhaps it may be argued that there are some rulers who deserve to be deprived of that right because they impede the spiritual good by preventing bishops from going to the Roman curia when they have been summoned on spiritual business or when it is necessary for them or for others to go there for dispensation from some irregularity or for some

[3] *De sacramentis* 2.2.4 PL 176.420. The scriptural text cited is Matth. 22.21.

similar cause. For it is evident that to impede a journey of this kind is to obstruct the spiritual good. Furthermore, such travel restrictions, as well as laws preventing money from leaving the kingdom, inflict damage on the Roman curia. The pope therefore has a legitimate grievance, and may forbid such laws and account a prince who acts so as his enemy. This is my answer: an unqualified prohibition and general ban on anyone wishing to make any sort of journey, would be to obstruct the spiritual good incidentally. But if the prohibition is of a limited nature, namely only imposed for reasonable cause by licence of the prince who has jurisdiction, there is no obstruction of the spiritual good. If such restrictions cause damage to the Roman curia, through loss of its accustomed dues, the prince should not be held to be acting unjustly or as an enemy to the Church, unless his intention is solely that of causing harm. For he is allowed to impose such rules, if it is for his personal good or the good of his country, even if it brings harm to others, since everyone is entitled to the benefit of his own right. The argument to establish this principle is: a man has a spring rising on his farm which divides into streams and irrigates the gardens of his neighbours. He then makes the water rise and channels it through different places of his home, whereby its course is diverted so that it no longer flows to his neighbours' gardens. Is he allowed to do this? The law says that his action is quite legal, even though some inconvenience may be caused to others, because he is taking advantage of his own right. Supposing however, that the prince does impose the restrictions with the intention of doing harm, even so, in exceptional circumstances his action may be legal; circumstances, that is, when he is persuaded by probable or evident arguments that the pope wishes to become his enemy or that he is summoning the prelates in order to conspire with them against the king or his kingdom. The prince is permitted to withstand the abuse of the spiritual sword as best he may, even by the use of the material sword, especially when abuse of the spiritual sword conduces to the mischief of the community whose care rests on the king. Otherwise he would be 'bearing the sword in vain'.[4]

38.   Concerning collation to benefices.

It must be noted that collation can be within the competence of a layman on the basis of custom, just as much as can presentation on the basis of written law; he is not the more excluded from the one than from the other. Also within his competence is right of patronage if established by valid custom, or grant by churches. As is said in *Ethics* 8 about what is due to a benefactor: if he is rich, respect is his due, if poor, payment of money; the obligation does not derive from a legal debt, from which legal actions between men arise, but from debt of honour.[5] Thus, in the beginning, churches were not bound by any legal obligation to their founders and patrons because of their benefactions, yet from a sense of obligation in honour, churches wished to grant their benefactors some mark of respect and some advantage. Presentation to benefices is then a way by which respect is accorded and can be found in written law as conceded to all patrons. Similarly for conferring of benefices on suitable candidates, with clerical advice. Although this is not to be found conceded to patrons in written law expressly and generally,

[4] Rom. 13.4.
[5] Cf. Ethics 8.14.

yet it is wholly granted and reasonably so, to certain distinguished patrons, the better to foster their devotion in founding churches. What has been granted reasonably, even though by favour and not as a legal obligation, is converted by long prescriptive custom into common right; as Plato says in the *Timaeus,* when one something has been rationally established, it is not God's will for it to be changed.[6] For this reason, presentation to ecclesiastical benefices is due in general to all patrons, and collation is owed specifically to certain eminent individuals who have acquired this right lawfully by custom. It cannot therefore be taken from them without injury. It is unquestionably wrong for anyone without evident and reasonable cause to seek to deprive them; the right to collate remains the patron's whatever anyone attempts against it. For, as has been said earlier,[7] God did not give the power of administering ecclesiastical property to Peter and the ministers of the Church, not to destroy it, as the Apostle says in the last chapter of 2 Corinthians.[8] For God does not want anyone to be deprived of what has been properly conferred on him, unless it be for some fault, since according to the Apostle, Romans 11: 'The gifts of God are without repentance',[9] and in Job 36 it is written: 'He will not take away his eyes from the just; and he placeth kings on the throne for ever'.[10] Because of the sins of the Egyptians, he made their vessels the spoils of the Jews.[11]

---

[6] Cf. Plato, *Timaios* c.10, 13.
[7] Cf. c.6 above.
[8] 2 Cor. 13.10.
[9] Rom. 11.29.
[10] Job 36.7.
[11] Cf. Exodus 12.35-36.

There can be no doubt that Christ did not give the pope power to revoke right of collation without evident and serious fault, in which the prince having first been admonished has been found incorrigible. This follows from the fact that it was conceded from the beginning to patrons, either expressly or implicitly through long neglect, and for reasonable cause, as also because of that obligation in honour by which respect is owed to a distinguished benefactor and as an encouragement to men of substance to endow churches. It has been precisely from this practice that the churches have benefited considerably.

To the argument that collation does not fall within the power of a layman since it is a spiritual matter, my reply is: it should be understood that nothing can be described as spiritual in the strict sense unless its relationship to the divine spirit is through causality or concomitance. Thus the sacraments of the Church are spiritual as is their administration, because they contain grace and cause it. Something is deemed to be annexed to the spiritual which is related to a given spiritual thing: either by consequence, as is right to tithe, or by antecedence, as is right of patronage and of collation of prebends. The first category, the strictly spiritual, can belong to a layman in no way at all. Neither can the second, that is, what is annexed to it by way of consequence, because such depends on spiritual function; it is by virtue of spiritual function that right to tithe is held. Thus, since spiritual function is not for laymen, neither is this right, though the material fruits called tithe may belong to a layman by grant of the Church. But the third category, namely, what is annexed to spiritual function by way of antecedence, such as presentation or collation or right to confer, can belong to a layman, because the dependence is not on the spiritual, but the other way round. A king can acquire such a right for himself, especially by grant or permission of the Church or through long standing prescriptive right. For this is not inconsistent with his status; if it were, there is no one empowered to concede it to him, just as there is no authority which could permit a layman to administer the sacraments or hold right of tithe. This is not burdensome for churches but is often fruitful, especially when done with the knowledge and permission of the Church.

To the argument that an endowment ought not to constitute a burden, I reply that the only way this endowment becomes burdensome is for the patron himself, who bears the burden of Church defence. In truth, it is not just burdensome, since the Church has more from it of advantage than disadvantage.

To the argument that custom should not prejudice public law, I reply that this custom, since it is not very harmful to the ministers of the Church but is in many ways fruitful, does not prejudice public law *in genere,* though it does seem to prejudice it *in specie.* For though it seems to be prejudicial to bishops who are deprived of that collation to benefices which public law allows them, yet in other ways, churches receive even more than is lost, in defence, endowment and foundation; therefore it is not a simple case of prejudice. Or as the Philosopher says in *Ethics* 8, we do this ourselves, because we do it through friends.[12] Thus it is the churchman who is said to confer, though not by his own agency but through the lay patron, to whom, on

---

[12] Cf. *Nic. Ethics* 8.13.

reasonable grounds, he has conceded the right. This concession is revocable only in the circumstances I have outlined earlier.

To what is said about custom contrary to the substance of a contract and being unethical, I say that no condition or contract is in question here, for patrons do not give conditionally or relatively but without reserve, although obligation follows once the collation is performed. There is nothing unethical either, since the right was not wrested violently from the Church but was freely granted to patrons by the Church; granted from that obligation in honour by which respect is due to every benefactor of superior rank and payment of money to one in need, as is said in *Ethics* 8.[13] Even if the custom were contrary to the substance of contract or gift, as the argument claims, it does not therefore follow that it should now be considered as inapplicable and that the gift does not remain valid. For this would be a question of unethical condition which is not contrary to the essence of the contract: as, for example, if it were said, I will marry you, if you kill a man. Where, however, the condition posed is contrary to the essence of the gift, the gift or contract is invalid: as, for example, if it were said, I will marry you, if you make yourself sterile by taking poison, or some comparable vitiation of the essence of the contract. A donation made to churches carrying a vitiating condition of this sort would be invalid and what was conferred should revert to the donors.

To the argument that the Church has the legal status of a minor and considers itself to have been deceived, I

---

[13] Cf. *ibid.* 8.14.

answer that it does not suffice for restitution merely to be a minor unless injury can be proved, D.54 *c. Generalis.*[14] The Church certainly cannot do this since it is obvious that it has been enriched by this permission. Further, eminent jurists maintain that the Church is considered to have just completed twenty six of its thirty year minority at the time of the infliction of the injury, so that restitution may only be made within a four year period, called the time of advantage, and within that period only, not after it, unless it is proved that fraud has had a part. Others say that restitution should be allowed for up to fifteen years, with the Church's period of minority fourteen years, but others allow up to thirty years, putting the Church at the beginning of its thirty year minority. Further, Goffredus says that the Church differs from a minor in this: the Church can claim prescriptive right, and be claimed against; whereas a minor is always kept unimpaired, (except by very long prescription, which does run against a minor but with right of restitution); prescription of forty year term runs against the Church, without right of restitution.[15]

39.   The pope ought to be self-sufficient in the active life.

This obligation concerns only the disposition of his personal affairs not those of others and also the instruction of others as to how they should distribute what they have according to the dictates of the order of charity.

40.   Clergy are stronger in intellectual power.

If this is so, they ought not therefore to dominate in

---

[14] *Decretum* D.54 c.12.
[15] Goffredius de Trani, *Summa super titulis decretalium tit. De in integrum restitutione* (1.41).

everything but only in the higher and the better, namely, in spiritual matters.

41. Those who speak otherwise are speaking in flattery of princes.

In some circumstances, it is permissible to conceal the truth, as Moses did in the issue of repudiating a wife, as Matthew 19 says.[16] But it is never permissible in any circumstances to teach or write against one's conscience in a matter of religious doctrine. Therefore, to say that men of eminence, popes among them, have written against their conscience to win the favour of princes, or through fear of them, is to 'set the mouth against heaven'.[17] It is probably nearer the mark to say that quite the contrary is the case: these doctors who so unduly extend the pope's authority, are speaking in fear or favour of the pope, since they are churchmen whose careers the pope could advance. Especially so, since they themselves claim, though wrongly, that the pope graciously embraces those who extend his power and censures those who speak against him, which kings and princes do not do.

42. Henry of Cremona's argument that they should be considered heretics who say the pope has not universal power in temporal affairs etc.

It must be said at the outset that his judgment is rash when he makes us say that the Church cannot coerce heretics. For such an opinion would appear false from the evidence that the Church can invoke the secular arm against heretics, as given in *Extra. De hereticis c. Ad*

16 Matth. 19.8.
17 Ps. 72.9.

abolendam and *c. Vergentis.*[18] It must be said that it is
rather he who incurs anathema and who is not far from
heresy, if he persists with his assertion. For there is
nothing in Scripture, which is the rule of faith, to say that
the pope has both swords. In Deuteronomy 4 the Lord
says: 'You shall not add to the word that I speak to you:
neither shall you take away from it'.[19] In the *Acts of the
First Council of Ephesus,* it is said that 'after the Nicene
creed had been recited, the holy synod ordered that no one
would be permitted to utter, draw up or put together any
declaration of faith other than that defined by the
holy fathers assembled by the Holy Spirit in Nicea
and added the sanction of anathema'; the same is
repeated in the *Acts of the Council of Chalcedon.*[20]
Moreover, since the Christian faith is catholic and universal,
the pope cannot make this binding in faith without a
general council, because a pope cannot destroy the decrees
of a council, as D.19 *c. Anastasius*[21] states. For although
a council cannot impose a law on a pope, *Extra. De
electione c. Significasti*[22] and 35.q. 9 *c. Veniam,*[23] yet this is
not to be interpreted as referring to what concerns the
faith. For as to that, the world is greater than the city,
and pope with council is greater than the pope alone,
D.93 *c. Legimus.*[24]

---

[18] *Decretales* 5.7.9, 10.
[19] Deut. 4.2.
[20] Dom Leclercq suggests Aquinas, *Summa theologiae* 2-2.q.1 a.10, obj. 2
as the source for the Acts of these councils.
[21] *Decretum* D.19 c.9.
[22] *Decretales* 1.6.4.
[23] *Decretum* 35 q.9 c.5.
[24] *Decretum* D.93 c.24. Presumably 'the city' is Rome.

CHAPTER XXI

*The Donation of Constantine and what the
pope can do in consequence of it.*

It has been seen what the ministers of the Church can
do by virtue of their position as vicars of Christ. It remains now to examine what popes can do by virtue of the
gift of Emperor Constantine the Great. For it is claimed
that he gave the western empire to Silvester and his
successors and the imperial emblems such as his palace,
crown and the like. Some people propose therefore that
by reason of this gift, the pope is emperor and lord of the
world and that he can appoint kings and get rid of them
like an emperor, especially during a vacancy of empire and
that he can be appealed to, just like an emperor. But to
make matters clearer, there must be set out the relevant
facts concerning this donation and translation of the empire,
as they are recorded in the chronicles and ancient histories.
It will then be possible to form a better appreciation of
what authority the pope may have by virtue of the
donation, particularly over the king of France.

It must be understood then of the above said donation
that on the evidence of Hugh of Fleury's *Chronicle,* of the
Cosmography, of Constantine's *Letter to the bishops,* and
of *The Testament* of *Constantine,*[1] Constantine only dona-
ted one province, namely Italy, along with certain other
territories, not including France, and translated the empire
to the Greeks, where he built a New Rome. About the

[1] Cf. Vincent of Beauvais, *Speculum historiale* 13.57 for these sources. The
rest of the donation is given, *Decretum* D.96 c.14 (Palea).

alleged translation of the empire from Greeks to Germans, made by the Romans and the pope, in the person of Charlemagne, it must be understood that these same chronicles make it clear that the translation was of such a nature that the substance of the empire remained Greek, whilst its title became western. Another way of looking at it is: a division was made whereby two emperors were named, one at Rome, the other at Constantinople. The Romans, it may be read, seceded from the Greeks for three reasons: for the defence of the republic they had accepted from Charlemagne when the emperor Constantine was negligent; because they were provoked to hatred of Empress Irene who blinded her son Constantine and her grandsons, in order to secure the empire for herself alone; because they were angered and chagrined at Constantine's transference of the empire from themselves to the Greeks. Hence they chanted the imperial praises for the victorious Charles. These considerations make it clear that the donation and translation confer no power on the pope over the king of France. There are four reasons to be considered.

Firstly, the donation affected only a specified portion of the empire, in which France was not included. The translation made to the Germans was not of the whole empire or monarchy of the world, since even after the translation, which was more a division of the empire or a new name for it than a true translation, the emperors still remained Greek.

Secondly, the donation was invalid, for the four reasons given by the Gloss on the Civil Law,[2] which represents the common opinion of legal experts.

---

[2] Cf. Accursius ad *Nov.* 6 pr. *s.v. conferens generi.*

(i) The emperor is called always 'augustus' because it is his continual task to augment the empire, not to diminish it. Thus it seems that the donation ought not to have held good, especially since it was immoderately huge, when otherwise, as moderate remuneration, it might have been valid. This argument is based on *De tutoribus l. Cum plures,*[3] and laws following. It is not an objection that the law says that the measure of donation to the Church is immensity, as *Authentica, De rebus ecclesie non alienandis § Sancimus.*[4] For this law is to be understood with reference to a gift from the patrimony which the emperor possessed before he became emperor, not to what is given from the public treasury, which [because it is established for the public good and by the community],[5] ought always to continue; grants ought only to be made from it under control and for certain reasons, as *Authentica, Quomodo oporteat episcopos et clericos* coll.2.[6] Or again: its reference is to the circumstances where a prince is making an exchange for Church property, not making a gift; a circumstance where there is no danger if the property of the prince is the greater and not commensurate with what he gets from the Church.

(ii) The emperor is administrator of the empire and the republic, as the laws decree, especially the Hortensian law, *Instituta, De constitutionibus principum l.1.*[7] But if he is

---

[3] Digest 27.7.12.

[4] Nov. 6.1.

[5] This sentence is an addition to some manuscripts. It is added here because it expresses one of John of Paris's most characteristic emphases, the common good, and throws light on one of the sources of his thinking on this principle.

[6] Nov. 6.3.

[7] Digest 1.4.1.

the administrator of the empire, the donation does not hold good, as *Instituta, Pro emptore, l. Qui fundum § Si tutor.*[8]

(iii) To give in this way constitutes a law, *Codex, De donatione inter virum et uxorem l. Donationes.*[9] But a law made by one emperor can be revoked by his successor, because an equal does not have command over equal, as *Instituta, De arbitris l. Nam et magistratus.*[10] Therefore this donation was not durable.

(iv) If one emperor can donate one part, a successor can donate another part and thus the empire is diminished and despoiled. This is inappropriate to its status, for the law states that it is expedient for the empire to be strong in possessions, as *Instituta, De fundamentis domorum l. Scilicet;*[11] *Authentica, Ut iudices suffraganei § Cogitatio* coll. 2.[12] Hence the jurists maintain that the donation was invalid.

The donation was displeasing to God. This may be gathered from the statement in the *Life of Pope St Sylvester* that at the time of the donation, angelic voices were heard on high to say: 'This day poison has been spread abroad in the Church'. Again, St Jerome says of Constantine that pillage of churches and dissension in the whole world has succeeded him right down to his own time. Jerome also says of him that afterwards he turned to such cruelty as to kill his son Crispus and his own wife Fausta. In the last hours of his life, he was baptized by Eusebius

---

[8] Digest 41.4.7.3.
[9] Code 5.16.25.
[10] Digest 4.8.4.
[11] *Recte* Digest 1.18.20.
[12] *Nov.* 8 Pr.

bishop of Nicomedia and so was baptized a second time; furthermore he lapsed into Arian doctrine. Many truthful and reliable writers say the same in their chronicles. Some people wish to defend Constantine by saying these things should be understood of his son. But this is false, for Jerome later on said sufficient about that son for there to be no confusion. It is generally agreed that pillage of churches did not begin with the second Constantine just because there was in his time a great persecution of the Church. It is also agreed from the *Chronicles* that only Constantine, not his son, had a wife called Fausta. The second Constantine is not found to have been a friend of Bishop Eusebius of Nicomedia. It was the other Constantine who was buried in his own church, and so Jerome and others speak of those crimes as attributable to Constantine the Great, although his spirit of piety led St Gregory, in his Register,[13] to hold him in happy memory. The Greeks too, have conceived a devotion for him because he transferred the empire to them and founded Constantinople in their midst.

Thirdly, even granting the validity of the donation and its general applicability to the empire as a whole, it is clear that it gives the pope no power over the king of France. For although it can be discovered of the Gauls that they are subject in certain respects to the Romans at the time of Emperor Octavian, the Franks never were subject. What can be read in various histories is how, after the fall of Troy, twelve thousand Trojans under the leadership of Athenon, after whom at first they were

[13] *Ep*. 5.39 PL 77.163.

named Athenorids, came to Pannonia and built the city of Sycambria beside the Melotis marshes. They were always hostile to the Roman empire. There they remained until the time of the emperor Valentinian who expelled them from those parts, because they refused to pay the Romans the taxes paid by other nations. They moved out under the leadership of Marcomirus, Surmo and Gennebaldus and settled on the bank of the Rhine on the border of Germania and Alemania. After the same Valentinian had tried unsuccessfully and after heavy fighting to conquer them, he gave them a name of their own, Franks, meaning 'fierce'. From that time, the military skill of the Franks so developed that they conquered the whole of Germany and Gaul right up to the summits of the Pyrenees and beyond, and living in Gaul, which they called France, were subject neither to the Romans nor to anybody else.[14]

Fourthly, granting again that the donation was valid and was made of the whole empire and granting, in addition, that the Franks were then subject to the empire (which we do not admit), nevertheless it gives no power over the kingdom of France to the pope. For he is not the emperor. But granting that he were the emperor, the Franks were exempt by prescription from imperial jurisdiction down to the time in question. Thus kings of sanctity ruled the kingdom of France over a long period of time and in good faith as, for example, St Louis who was canonized by the Church for his obvious merits: he held the kingdom and the Church, in canonizing him, has approved the fact, whatever some theologians say. For acquisition of property

[14] Some of this was possibly taken from Godfrey of Viterbo's *Pantheon* pt. 17 (PL 198.919).

and subjection of men are a matter for human law; according to Augustine, it is the human laws which make property common or belong to individuals, and can take away what is mine for reasonable cause and transfer lordship.[15] Thus imperial laws have decreed that anything transferred after so long a time by prescription is transferred as ownership. This is permitted for the common welfare or in despite of a negligent owner and in approbation of the good faith of the possessor, to prevent the multiplication of lawsuits and their indefinite protraction. Nor, in this context, does anyone hold the property of another; it is his own, made such by lawful prescription. So then, even when it is conceded that at some earlier time the kingdom of France was subject to the Roman empire, yet that subjection has been abolished by prescription. This emerges from the *Chronicles* of Sigebert and of others. For it can be read that Charlemagne brought all Italy under the sway of the king of the Franks. It can be read also in the *Chronicles of the Romans* that formerly the empire was held by the Franks, yet everyone would agree that Italy is not now subject to the French.[16] Such a change would be impossible except for the operation of prescription over a period of time which has its place in such issues.

From all that has been said so far, it is evident that some lawyers are wrong when in speaking of prescription of jurisdiction over subjects. They say that it is only subjection to inferior barons, not subjection to the emperor, that can be prescribed, so that there is always subjection

---

15 Cf. *Decretum* D.8 c.1.
16 Vincent of Beauvais, *Speculum historiale* 23.169.

to the superior. Their argument is that since a multitude of people will easily fall into disagreement, it is inexpedient to let a multitude have governmental power: one man should be head of the whole world. Therefore this advantage shall not be removed by prescription. But this argument carries little conviction, as is evident from what was said earlier in chapter 3. It is true that a multitude will readily disagree in any single issue and so a regal constitution is better than an aristocratic one, as was said in chapter 1 above. Yet it is better that many should rule in many kingdoms than one alone should rule the whole world.

This is made clear from the fact that the world was never as peaceful in the time of the emperors as it was beforehand and afterwards. Brother would murder brother and mother her son and *vice versa*, while dreadful crimes and great strife ran riot throughout the world, details of which are unnecessary here. It would be astounding if, as the claim is, prescription did not run against the Roman empire since there were other empires before it: the Babylonian, beginning with Ninus in the time of Abraham, the Carthaginian, under Cola, at the time of Judges, the Macedonian or Greek, beginning with Alexander at the time of Maccabees. Each of these empires was just as much from God as the Roman empire.

If then, notwithstanding the divine origin of the empire of the Greeks, the Romans could exempt themselves from their rule and try to usurp the empire by expelling them, why cannot other men make prescription against the Roman empire, even by revolt, especially when submission to Roman rule was imposed on them by force, against their will? Just as is read of the Gauls that before the Franks

came, they never voluntarily submitted to the Romans,
but were always in revolt as best they could, sometimes overcoming the Romans, sometimes being overcome by them. If then the Romans achieved dominion by force, it is not just that their dominion can be
thrown off by force, or that prescription should run against
them?

If anyone were to say it was God's providence for other
empires to come to an end, while that of the Romans continued to grow, why cannot it be argued along similar lines
about the Roman empire, that in God's providence, it too
should come to an end and those who were formerly in
any way subject to it, cease to be so and if they have the
will and the ability, break the connexion altogether? In
fact, it seems to be quite expressly stated in Scripture
that the Roman empire should fail just like any other.
For it is said in Numbers 24 in the prophecy of Balaam:
'They shall come in galleys from Italy: they shall overcome
the Assyrians, and shall waste the Hebrews: and at the
last they themselves also shall perish'.[17] The Master commenting on this text in his *Histories* observes: 'Just as he
predicted the monarchy of the Romans, so also he foretold
their destruction at the last'.[18] Similarly in Daniel, in the
context of the vision of the four great beasts, on the text
where reference is made to the fourth beast which shall
tread down the whole world, the Gloss comments that
'nothing was stronger than the kingdom of the Romans and
nothing, in the end, shall be more feeble or more
perishable'.[19]

[17] Num. 24.24.
[18] Petrus Comestor, *Historia scholastica*, *Lib. num.* c.33 PL 198.1239.
[19] Dan. 7.23 and *glossa ordinaria*.

CHAPTER XXII

Whether it is lawful to debate and make judgment about these issues concerning the pope

It would now seem appropriate to enquire whether or not it is blameworthy to make judgment about papal acts, since some people say that to do this is as if 'to touch the sacred mountain'[1] and to 'set the mouth against heaven'.[2] They also say that Dioscorus was condemned forever by a general council for criticizing Pope Leo and wishing to judge him.[3]

Discussion and judgment of papal conduct may be classified under four headings: status, power, abuse of power, personal defect. Concerning the status of a pope, that is, whether he is pope or not, I maintain that it is lawful to question and discuss. For there may be doubt because of electoral defect. The election is conducted according to a fixed procedure, in which error can occur, just as it can in the election of any other prelate. Again, it is valid to examine the question of status on account of personal defect because it might be necessary to remove someone from the see, a woman or a heretic for example, as were some in the past, whose names for this reason do not appear in the catalogue of popes. The more dangerous it is not to know the truth, the more it is necessary to find

---

[1] Cf. Exodus 19.12.
[2] Ps. 72.9.
[3] *Decretum* D.21 c.9.

out the truth. In such cases, however, this must be observed, that no groundless and trivial objections be entertained, by taking into account when and by whom objections are put forward. If after careful examination of the person and election of a pope by learned men and others involved, something impermissible touching his status is found, there must be no covering up. He must be advised to withdraw. If he is unwilling to do so, he can be taken captive, a general council called and the case laid before it. If in such a case, he proves obstinate and violent he ought to be removed, even with the aid of the secular arm, lest the sacraments of the Church be profaned.[4]

Thus the *Chronicles of the Roman Pontiffs* record the deposition through the praiseworthy intervention of the secular power, of Benedict IX and Cadelus bishop of Porto, of Constantine II and of others who had forced their way into office.[5] But who will judge a pope to be heretical? My answer is: if he has said something contrary to what the professions of faith officially approved by the Church contain, and maintains it by affirmation, then he is said to be already judged, for 'he that doth not believe is already judged'.[6]

About the power of the pope, that is, about what he can and cannot do, I believe it not to be blameworthy to seek the truth. For ignorance here is dangerous and there is an element of uncertainty about some issues, for example,

---

[4] John of Paris here goes far towards anticipating principles urged and in part adopted in practice in the crisis of the Great Schism, 1378-1415.
[5] Vincent of Beauvais, *Speculum historiale*.
[6] John 3.18.

whether the pope can dispense a bigamist or whether he can dispense from a solemn vow of celibacy, when it is found that in practice one pope at some time has dispensed, while another pope says he has no power to do so, *Extra, De ingredientibus monasterium.*[7] There are many doubts, even numberless doubts, concerning papal power about which it is advantageous to deliberate and even, as seems reasonable to any individual, humbly come to a decision.

About abuse of power and personal defect, for example, whether he confers prebends for the common need of the Church or for his own private advantage, or whether he is chaste or sober or criminal, if it is not obvious and palpable, there can be no doubt that it is not lawful to judge. Interpretation must always incline towards giving him the benefit of the doubt, even if on the face of things, there appears to be some taint of evil; it is much less lawful to judge of the pope than of others. If something which is intrinsically wrong has been committed like incontinence or murder or what is forbidden by the law, he cannot be judged through the action of another authority bringing him to court and excommunicating him, for he has no superior. Hence Dioscorus who excommunicated Pope Leo, as is recounted in D.21, was condemned forever by a general council. Some also say that he should not be judged through the procedure of simple judgment and correction, because if we interpret the murder of Samson, which is evil in itself, as having been done by divine inspiration, much more ought we to interpret every action of the most holy father as good and if the sin of theft or some-

---

[7] There is no such title in the *Decretales*. Cf. 1.21.2 and *glossa ordinaria* for a discussion that would fit this context.

thing else intrinsically evil has been committed, we ought
to view it as happening by inspiration of God whose will
and guidance direct holy church rather than any individual
person. But St Augustine makes a good enough answer in
his *City of God* Book 1.[8] For, as he says, we interpret the
murder of Samson as having been prompted by God, because he worked other miracles through him. Thus, in
my view, when a pope palpably does wrong, for example,
by depriving churches of their rights, by dispersing the
Lord's flock, by scandalizing the Church through some act
of his, he can be judged, prevailed upon and censured by
anyone at all, not in virtue of their office but in ardour of
charity, and not with imposition of punishment but with
reverent exhortation. For the love which every person is
owed, is not less owed by reason of the greater position
to which he has been raised. Thus the pope is not less
owed the compassion of charity because of his position, but
while heedful of authority, according to Augustine, everyone is bound under the obligation of charity to fraternal
correction of one who does wrong; the obligation to show
the compassion of charity is not the less for its recipient
being the pope, though it must be shown with humility and
reverence. Hence when Peter had come to Antioch, Paul
withstood him to his face because he was blameworthy.[9]
It cannot be said then that to speak out in this context is
to 'touch the sacred mountain' or 'set the mouth against
heaven', because when a pope manifestly offends that is
not heaven, nor when he is corrected can it be said
that the mouth is being set against him; rather is it for him.

[8] Cf. *De civitate Dei* 1.21 (CSEL 40.5.1.39-40).
[9] Cf. Gal. 2.11.

No one should fear that on this account scandal would touch the pope, for general scandal does not bother grown men, only children. Hence to fear scandal about the pope in this respect is to hold the pope to be childish, less mature than someone whom others dare to correct when he does wrong; therefore in truth, it is these people who 'set their mouths against heaven', in saying about the most holy father such things as that he is revengeful and acts harshly towards anyone who judges anything of what he does. This view certainly should not be held, since he is not a man of petty spirit but is righteous, and more righteous than others.

What if the pope were to announce that he considered any man a heretic who maintained a certain opinion about which the learned differ and were to make this pronounce-ment without a general council? For example, if he were to say that he considers every person who denies the temporal subjection of the king of France and similar dignitaries to himself as a heretic? I reply that words spoken by a pope without precision should, as far as possible, always be given a reasonable meaning. Thus the pronouncement should not be interpreted as meaning that appeal can be made to him in temporal matters or that he has lordship in temporal property or that he can intervene to decide disputes of property possession. This inter-pretation would be obviously contrary to Scripture and commonly accepted doctrine and would constitute a novelty of a kind which the pope should only put forward after deep deliberation, the holding of a general council and discussion by the learned everywhere. Therefore, having regard to how he has disclosed his mind on the matter, the pronouncement ought to be interpreted in this reasonable sense: the subjection referred to is subjection by reason of crime, that is, in an issue concerning sin, or further, it should be understood with reference to the forum of conscience, as was said earlier. Should he finally disclose, however, that he intended a novel and injurious meaning (perish the thought), he must be endured in patience, as far as this is possible without endangering justice and truth, in the spirit of Matthew 5: 'And whosoever will force thee one mile, go with him the other two'.[10] Recourse must be had to God who, having in his hand the heart of the pope, just as he has the heart of a king, can bring about change of heart in him. So too can he remove a pope, just as he can remove a king from his throne. If, however, there lies danger to society in delay, because the people are being led into evil opinion and there is danger of rebellion, and if the pope should disturb the people unduly by abuse of the spiritual sword, if there is no hope that he will otherwise desist, then I consider that the Church ought to move into action against him. The prince acting with moderation may resist the violence of the papal sword with his own sword. In this he does not act against the pope as pope but against an enemy of himself and of society, just as Aod the Israelite who slew Eglon king of Moab with the dagger he had tucked away against his thigh because he oppressed God's people in harsh servitude, was not considered to have killed a ruler but a wicked man who was an enemy.[11] This was not action against the Church, but for it. So the people,

---

[10] Matth. 5.41.
[11] Cf. Judges 3.16-22.

fired by the ardour of faith, commendably deposed Pope
Constantine, a source of scandal to the Church, and put
out his eyes. So too the emperor Henry going to Rome
deposed by imperial and canonical sanction Benedict IX
and two others whose contentions for the papacy scan-
dalized the Church, and made Clement II pope of the
Roman Church, as may be read in the *Chronicles of the
Romans.*

CHAPTER XXIII

The worthless arguments of those who maintain that the pope cannot resign

Now because earlier I seemed to assume that a pope can abdicate and be deposed and while alive no longer be pope after having been pope, we must see what arguments are used by those people who claim that the pope cannot voluntarily resign nor be deposed by the sole authority of lower prelates. There are listed in this and the following chapter, the arguments in support of the two articles clearly laid out above at the beginning of this treatise. For there are many arguments to be urged on both sides.

Here are the reasons given for not allowing papal resignation.

1. The pope cannot resign because the papacy is from God alone. But what comes from God, or is entrusted to anyone by an authority higher than his own, cannot be taken away by a lower authority. Thus, the papal dignity, committed to the pope by God, cannot be taken away by any authority lower than his.

2. No one can take away any authority or power which he cannot also confer. But no one save God can confer the papal authority. Therefore no one may take it away, which would be the position if the pope could resign.

3. The decretal *Inter corporalia*[1] expressly reserves the deposition, translation and absolution of bishops to the pope alone and that only in so far as he is God, i.e. the

[1] *Decretales* 1.7.2.

vicar of God. Therefore the removal of a pope from office can only be accomplished by God, since the papacy excels all other dignities and has no superior. For there seems no reason why God should wish bishops to be removable only by their superior, the pope, in so far as he is God, while allowing the pope himself to be removable by those inferior to him. Therefore it seems that it is God's will that only he can remove a pope who alone stands higher than a pope.

4. The highest virtue created cannot be taken away by any created virtue. But the papacy is the highest virtue created. Therefore the conclusion follows etc.

5. Neither the pope nor the whole universe of creation can bring about that a priest be made not a priest. Still less then can it be brought about that the supreme priest be the supreme priest no longer.

6. The pope is pope only by divine law and not at the same time through the law of any created being, or of all created beings together. Therefore it seems that the pope cannot in any way be exempted from being pope. From the fact that a pope agrees to be pope and subjects himself to the law of betrothal, he cannot be unmade as pope by any created being whether acting singly or in association with others.

7. No one can cancel anyone's vow except the man who is above the vow. But the papacy is a vow above all vows, because the pope vows to sustain the charge of the universal church and of the Lord's flock and because he will render account of it. Therefore any dispensation from that obligation must be by God himself. For someone bound to someone higher cannot absolve himself. Only the superior authority can absolve him.

8.   It would seem that no one is competent to absolve himself from sin, therefore neither can anyone absolve himself from the papacy: to concede that the pope could resign would be to concede the other.

9.   It would seem that the obligation to the papacy cannot be cancelled except by a power greater than papal power. But there is none higher except God's. Therefore the conclusion follows etc.

10.   Once canonical confirmation has taken place, no ecclesiastical dignity can be nullified except by the superior. But the pope has no superior other than God. Therefore the conclusion follows etc.

11.   The Apostle wants it that Christ's office as priest go on as long as he lives, that is, forever.[2] Therefore there cannot in any way be a living high priest without his holding the office of the highest priesthood, which would be false if the pope could resign.

These are the arguments relevant to the proposition that the pope cannot abdicate or be deposed.

---

[2] Cf. Heb. 7.24.

CHAPTER XXIV

Arguments that the pope can abdicate

Now we must show in numerous ways, that is, by examples, authorities and arguments from reason, that the pope can resign and even against his will, be deposed.

St Clement affords one example of abdication.[1] It can be read of him in the *Deeds of the Roman Pontiffs* that he abdicated and held the chair again after Linus and Cletus. He was thus the immediate successor of Peter, but on his resignation, Linus and Cletus held office. Clement resumed it after these popes and thereby was fourth in line from St. Peter. This example, however, may be a misrepresentation, since Aymo says in the *Record of Christian Affair*s and the same thing is said in certain other histories, that Linus and Cletus did not hold office as popes but were coadjutors of the pope in that St Peter in his own lifetime handed over to them the management of Church affairs, whilst he devoted himself entirely to prayer and preaching. Therefore since Linus and Cletus were endowed with such great authority, they deserved places in the catalogue of popes and so, according to these accounts, Clement did not resign but held the papal throne immediately after Peter, up to the reign of Anacletus or Evaristus.

[1] The primary source for these papal case histories is Aegidius Romanus, *De renunciatione papae* c.24 part 2. Probably it was Vincent of Beauvais, *Speculum historiale* which was used in support.

However, I consider the first view the more correct and
that Clement's reason for resigning was perhaps because he
was made pope by Peter in Peter's lifetime, as he himself
wrote to St James, bishop of Jerusalem. Another example
that can be adduced is the case of Marcellinus who lived
in the time of Diocletian. His resignation is recorded in
the Gloss on 7 q.1 *c. Non autem*;[2] in D.21 *c. Nunc
autem*,[3] it is said that he deposed himself. His abdication
was in a certain sense a deposition because as Huguccio[4]
repeats from the *Deeds of the Roman Pontiffs,* he passed
sentence on himself, in accusing and charging himself when
he stated: 'I, Marcellinus, because of the charge of idolatry
which I have unhappily committed, judge that I be condemned and deposed. I pronounce anathema also on
anyone who should give me burial'. St Cyriacus may be
put forward as another example. It may be read of him
that he was martyred with Ursula and eleven thousand
virgins. It is recorded that one night he received a
revelation that he would gain the palm of martyrdom along
with those virgins. Then he assembled the clergy and
cardinals and in their presence resigned his dignity and
office, despite everyone's reluctance, especially the cardinals'. Cyriacus is not listed in the catalogue of popes
however, because it used to be believed he resigned the
papacy not for piety but to seek delectation with the
virgins.

Scholarly authorities also establish the principle of the
permissibility of papal abdication. The Gloss on 7. q.1 *c.*

---

[2] *Decretum* 7 q.1 c.12.

[3] *Decretum* D.21 c.7.

[4] The citations of Huguccio are taken from A. Romanus, *De renunciatione
papae* c.24 part 2.

Non autem raises the issue squarely with the question of whether a pope may resign, and answers in the affirmative, explaining that Marcellinus and even Clement resigned. Huguccio, too, in the same place, asks: 'But what of the resignation of a pope? Can he resign because he wants to join a religious order or because he is ill or old'? His answer is that he most certainly can resign, giving the abdications of Marcellinus and Clement as his reason. Similarly at D.21 *c. Nunc autem,* he asks the same question and replies that a pope can abdicate if it is expedient to do so: if it is not, and he abdicates, he commits sin.

Arguments from reason, discussing the matter in terms of final cause, can also be adduced to establish the same conclusion. No one is chosen to be pope for any reason other than the common good of the Church and the Lord's flock. The end of his ruling activity is the common benefit. If therefore, after taking up office, he should find himself, or be found to be, totally unsuitable or useless, or if some impeding condition such as insanity occurs later, he ought to seek release from the people or from the college of cardinals, which in this case stands in the place of the whole clergy and people. Whether permission is obtained or not, he should abdicate. For otherwise, if he could not resign, what was instituted in charity, would be warring against charity, should he continue to rule injuriously, causing evil and confusion in the Church and imperilling his own soul. It is a general truth that no obligation voluntarily undertaken can be prejudicial to that duty in charity by which everyone is bound to look to the salvation of his own soul, even as a religious who makes profession within a prescribed rule may freely transfer to a stricter rule if it should seem expedient for himself and his salvation, whether permission of his superior has been granted or not. As 19 q.2 *c. Due sunt leges* states in this context: 'there is no reason why a man who is guided by private law should be constrained by public law'.[5] Therefore if after careful examination, there is discovered to be weakness of spirit or folly which is a scandal to the Church or anything which disturbs the Church or disunites the Lord's flock, and if admonition is ignored, then he must be compelled to resign, in accordance with the principles laid down in *Extra. De renunciatione c. Quidam cedendi* and *Cum in postulatione.*[6]

It is not, then, unreasonable to say that the pope can give up his position and abdicate even when the people do not want him to and demand him back, as in the case of St Cyriacus. It is not unreasonable to go further and say that in the case of his being unwilling, by consent of the people he can be deposed and compelled to resign. For the pope, like any other prelate, rules not for himself but for the benefit of the people. Therefore the consent of the people is of more significance for deposing him against his will should he seem wholly useless and for electing another, than the will of the pope to resign when the people are not agreeable to his doing so.

In deposition, where the removal from office is done against the pope's will and through the people, procedure must be more deliberate than in voluntary resignation. It suffices for abdication for the pope to lay his case before the college of cardinals who in this situation stand in the place of the whole Church. For deposition, however, a

[5] *Decretum* 19 q.2 c.2.
[6] *Decretales* 1.9.12. The reference is to this text only.

general council is more appropriate, as appears from D.21 *c. Nunc autem,* where it is said that a general council was summoned to depose Marcellinus. I believe, however, that the college of cardinals on its own is adequate to depose, for it would seem that the body whose consent, in place of the whole Church, makes a pope, might conversely, unmake him. If the cause be reasonable and sufficient, they earn merit by deposing him; if it is insufficient, they commit sin. To say that any of the points argued here do not hold against the pope because he has no superior except God, is invalid, as will appear in answering the arguments by which that proposition is urged.

CHAPTER XXV

Replies to the arguments given in Chapter 23.

1. That the papacy is from God alone.

It must be said that papal power can be considered in two ways. Firstly according to its own nature; in itself, it comes from God alone, because God alone can give this power to men, since that which is loosed or bound on earth, is loosed or bound in heaven. Secondly it may be considered as it is in this or that person; as such it is from God alone in the sense that we attribute all our actions to God, Isaias 26: 'Thou hast wrought all our works for us';[1] for it is he who works all things in all men, both to will and to accomplish.[2] Every work of ours is attributed to him alone if we do well, while if our work is defective, this is our own fault. What comes from God alone does not exclude action of our own, for we are cooperators with God. Thus although the papacy is itself from God alone, yet in so far as it is in this or that person, it comes through human cooperation, by way of the agreement of the man elected and the electors. On this line of reasoning, then, it can, by human agreement, cease to exist in this or that man. There is an analogy with the case of the rational soul which comes from God alone by creation, yet nature cooperates in the arrangement and organization of what is in the body. So then the rational

[1] Is. 26.12.
[2] Cf. Philip. 2.13.

soul can cease to exist in that body because of the working of nature, when natural warmth by consuming moisture has made the body unfit for a rational soul.

2. God alone can confer the papacy: he alone can take it away.

The answer here is the same as in the previous argument. A further example can be added. It is God alone who bestows grace, yet a man must cooperate in order to gain grace for, according to Augustine, he who has made you without your assistance, will not justify you without your assistance. Thus man by his own action can take away grace from himself.

3. Concerning the decretal *Inter corporalia* which reserves to the pope alone the deposition, translation and resignation of bishops.

This argument leads to the conclusion that the pope can resign without the authority of his superior rather than to the contrary conclusion. It is the natural order of things that the opposite of what established something, will destroy it. An example of this is the marriage between a prelate and his church. This is established by the consent of electors and elect and is therefore dissolved by their dissent. Hence any bishop who feels himself too weak, unsuitable or useless for the care of souls and the rule of his church would be able to resign, having put his case to the people or to his chapter, except that this is forbidden by his superior, who has specially reserved cases touching bishops and archbishops to his own jurisdiction, in that decretal *Inter corporalia.* Because there is no prohibition imposed on the pope similar to the one applicable to lesser bishops, the pope can resign and be deposed without the authority of any superior. For in such matters where action is according to the requirements of matter and cause, what is not forbidden, is lawful. But in those matters where action goes beyond the competence of the agent in matter or cause, nothing is lawful unless expressly granted. Such is the right to regulate churches which pertains to the pope as head of the Church and lies outside the competence of lesser bishops. Hence it is not lawful for any of these to act unless specially authorized to do so. The pope is not in a similar position, for there is no reservation for a superior. Resignation is not forbidden him as it is to inferior bishops whose resignations are reserved to a superior.

Another answer to this argument and others like it can be put forward: where there is manifest and reasonable cause, as when there is obvious defect, the consent and authority of God to the resignation and deposition may be supposed, just as divine consent is supposed when the one elected is confirmed in his office.

However, we must take into consideration a possible strengthening of the argument drawn from this decretal. The argument is: the decretal says that the spiritual bond between a bishop and his church is stronger than the physical bond between a man and his wife. If therefore the physical bond between man and wife cannot be dissolved by any human power or authority or consent of anyone at all, neither can the spiritual bond between pope and church. For in the episcopate, spiritual marriage is contracted with the election, ratified with the confirmation and consummated with the consecration. I reply to this: the spiritual bond is said to be stronger than the physical because it is more worthy, not because it is more durable. For a spiritual marriage can be dissolved even after the consecration of a bishop, if he is translated to another see, as stated in 7 q.1 *c. Mutationes* and *c. Pastoralis*,[3] or deposed, D.50 *c. Postquam*,[4] or resigns, as in many places of *Extra. De renunciatione*.[5] Such is not the case in physical marriage. Or again: the bond in spiritual marriage is said to be stronger because it binds and ties more tightly than the physical, not because it is to a greater degree indissoluble. For the care of a prelate for his church is the greater since his is for the common good, whereas that of a man for his wife is a particular good. Or again: it is said to be stronger because it is stronger in its nature than physical marriage. But that the physical is more durable, since the partners are not allowed to separate in their lifetime, comes most expressly from Christ's command to be found in the Gospel: 'What God has joined together, let no man put asunder'. Because of this Paul states: 'Not I, but the Lord commandeth that the wife depart not from her husband. And if she depart, that she remain unmarried or be reconciled to her husband'.[6] God forbade the dissolution of physical marriage because though it might foster a particular good it could work against the common good, since men might thereby be encouraged to get rid of their wives. The very opposite applies in spiritual marriage. For if a man who is incompetent and a source of scandal is not allowed to resign, or may not be deposed and another selected in his place, this state of affairs would be against the common good. For when such a person rules, his rule is solely for

---

[3] *Decretum* 7 q.1 c.34, 42.
[4] *Decretum* D.50 c.11.
[5] *Decretales* 1.9.
[6] 1 Cor. 7.10-11.

his own individual good. Therefore God has not forbidden it. If the legislator's reason for prohibiting the dissolution of physical marriage be properly understood, it will be understood why he commands spiritual marriage to be dissolved whenever it is obvious it stands in the way of the common good.

4. A pope cannot be deposed against his will because the papacy is the highest created excellence.

Here some would maintain that the argument leads to a true conclusion: although a pope can resign, he cannot, however, be deposed against his will, unless he is a heretic. In this case, he is considered to be dead and cannot therefore be head of the Christians. They prove this on the evidence of D.21 *c. Nunc autem*[7] which states that no one can with justice be submitted to the judicial decisions of those of lesser dignity and rank. This same canon says of Pope Marcellinus that no bishop dare pass sentence on him but they very frequently repeated to him: 'Judge your case on your own admission, not by our judgment' and again they charged him: 'Do not be heard according to our judgment' but put your case together in your own bosom' and yet again: 'You will be condemned out of your own mouth'. Hence his biography says that he deposed himself and was afterwards reinstated by the people. But I do not understand this line of argument. For a pope rules for the good of the Church and if, therefore, he can resign when the Church is unwilling, as was said of St Cyriacus, why can he not be deposed by the Church, even though he is unwilling, if there is sufficient reason?

[7] *Decretum* D.21 c.7.

Furthermore, in the special case of a church whose bishop is incapacitated by insanity either permanently or at intervals, should he refuse to resign when asked, another can and ought to be appointed, as 7.q.1. *c. Qualiter* and *c. Quamvis triste* with the gloss of Johannes Teutonicus thereon,[8] *Extra. De renunciatione c. Quidam cedendi.*[9] So likewise, the college of cardinals, acting in place of the whole Church, can depose a pope against his will.

Again, D.40 *c. Si papa*[10] states: 'He who will judge all must not be judged by anyone, unless he is caught deviating from the faith'. The Gloss comments here: if he is detected in some other crime, will not reform after admonition, is a cause of scandal to the Church and is incorrigible, then he can be brought to trial. For such contumacy is equivalent to heresy.

Again, if he can be deposed for heresy because thereby he is considered dead, why does not the same hold good if he falls into some other vice in which he reveals himself incorrigible? Such a man should also be considered dead and as counting for nothing, in accordance with St Augustine's dictum that sin is nothing and men are as nothing when they sin.[11] If there is refusal to resign when asked because of defect, another should be appointed because in that case, he would already appear to be acting wickedly.

When it is stated that the bishops did not dare to condemn Marcellinus, I reply that this was because he had been forced to his crime by Diocletian, he had repented and wished to be corrected and nothing had been proved

---

[8] *Decretum* 7 q.1 c.13, 14 and *glossa ordinaria.*

[9] *Decretales* 1.9.12.

[10] *Decretum* D.40 c.6 and *glossa ordinaria.*

[11] Cf. Sermo 169 c.11 PL 38.943.

against him except what of his own will he had confessed of himself and it was in this sense that he was judged out of his own mouth.

My answer to the claim in the principal argument that the papacy as the highest created excellence cannot be taken away is this: it is conceded that it is the highest in a person, yet there is an equal to him or even a greater, in the college of cardinals or in the whole Church. Or again: it may be said that he can be deposed by the college of cardinals or more so by a general council by the authority of God whose consent for deposition is supposed and presumed where there is manifest scandal and incorrigibility of its head.

5. Just as his priesthood cannot be taken away from a priest, so the high priesthood cannot be taken away from the chief priest.

The two cases are not similar. The words 'priest' and 'pontiff' have reference simply to what concerns the power of order, that is, the character of priesthood or the power founded on that character. This power operates in different ways. There is imprinted on the priest a character which is as if incomplete, for though his power of ministering the sacraments is based on it, yet he has no power to make another a priest with similar power of ministering the sacraments. There is conferred on a bishop, however, completeness of character and on it is grounded that complete sacerdotal power by virtue of which he has the power to make another person a priest. A bishop thus stands to a simple priest as an adult does to a youth. A bishop is not just any priest, he is a great priest, the spouse of his church, because he can, as it were, beget others of his kind through ordination of priests. An archbishop, a patriarch or primate, a pope do not derive from their titles, distinct from their priesthood and episcopacy, anything pertinent to the power of order or its augmentation or completion. Their titles express only degrees of jurisdiction going with the episcopate: an archbishop in his province, a primate in a kingdom, a pope in the whole Church. Because the power of order is indelible and its completion is indelible, in that it is founded on the character and on the completion of character, there is no agency by which a priest can be made not a priest, or a bishop not a bishop. But jurisdiction is another matter: just as it can be increased or diminished, so it can be deleted and taken away. Thus with his jurisdiction taken away from him, a pope ceases to be a pope, the high priest ceases to be high priest, but he does not cease to be a priest.

6. A pope only becomes such through the operation of divine law and not through the law of any created being or beings, and because of his subjecting himself to the law of betrothal, he cannot cease to be pope through any one created being or all of them together.

This argument rests on a double foundation. One is that the pope is pope by operation of the divine law which is immutable and therefore he cannot cease to be pope. The other is that he subjects himself to the law of betrothal that the Church may be perpetuated.

In answer to the first basic argument, it may be said that notwithstanding that the pope is pope through divine law which is immutable, nevertheless he can cease to be pope. For although divine law is unchangeable formally and in itself, like the law that inferiors are led to God through superiors and so inferior prelates through the pope, it is not unchangeable materially, in its application to this or that person, a Celestine or a Boniface, since as we have said, its application requires the cooperation of a created being. That the pope is above everyone is a rule of divine law and cannot be changed by anyone. But whether or not this or that individual is pope is changeable, because the consent of elect and electors cooperates in deciding on the choice of person.

In answer to the second basic argument, it may be said that the subjection of the pope to the law of his betrothal to the Church, which means that he is to be perpetuated in the Church with respect to the power of orders. He ought always to perform what pertains to him because of his spiritual marriage, namely, ordination, because when he ordains someone, the ordination is permanent. But as to what comes under the power of jurisdiction, he is not subject continuously and unalterably to the Church from the law of betrothal because jurisdiction can be taken away. The reason why what belongs to the power of order cannot be taken away and what is of the power of jurisdiction can be, is this: what is of jurisdiction is not supernatural and outside the ordinary operations of human affairs. For it is not beyond the ordinary condition of man that some men should have jurisdiction over others, for that is in a certain way natural. In such matters what is not forbidden is conceded; a thing is destroyed by the inversion of what had established it. So then, just as jurisdiction is conferred by consent of men, so contrariwise it may be taken away by consent. But what is pertinent to the power of order is above nature and the ordinary condition of things, since at the utterance of certain words, a character or spiritual power is imprinted on the soul. Therefore in such matters, what is not expressly granted, is denied. Hence because it is expressly assigned that a character is imprinted at the utterance of the words, therefore it is so. But because it is not found to be expressly laid down that it can in any way be removed, therefore the impression or imposition of a character on which is based the power of order, is indelible. Because, therefore, the pope subjects himself to the law of betrothal, his office is perpetual as far as those things pertaining to his order are concerned — to his priesthood, whereby he is marked by a certain character, and his episcopacy whereby that character is completed. But as to what is pertinent to the papacy or high priesthood, since the papacy and high priesthood add nothing except jurisdiction, it is not necessary for his office to be perpetual, since jurisdiction can be given up.

7. Concerning the vow taken by the pope.

The vow taken by the pope, namely, to undertake the universal care of the Lord's flock, must be understood as carrying the implication, so long as he will be in office, that is to say, as long as he will be pope. For it is thus that those who come to power in political societies bind themeslves to uphold the statutes of those societies and to keep them in good estate, all of which is understood to be applicable for as long as their term of office lasts. An oath by which a person swore that he would always be in such an office or in the papacy and that thus he had care of the people simply and absolutely for always would be unlawful, because it could militate against the common good, should he recognize his own incapacity and the resultant enfeeblement and collapse of the common good under his rule.

8. No one can absolve himself from sin.

The cases are not similar because to absolve oneself from sin is to ascend, but to absolve oneself from the papacy is to descend. The argument is not valid if it is proposing that a man cannot descend (i.e. resign the papacy) because he cannot ascend (i.e. forgive himself from sin). Or again: it can be said that man absolves himself from guilt through contrition and if he be obliged to confess afterwards to someone else from whom he receives absolution, this is solely because the Lord has commanded it, James 5: 'Confess therefore your sins one to another'[12] and in Luke 17 the Lord told the lepers, symbolizing sinners, to show themselves to the priests.[13]

9.   Papal obligation cannot be removed except by a greater power.

The reply is as given to other arguments. The pope's obligation is only conditional, relating only to his time in office.

10.   No ecclesiastical dignity can be annulled after canonical confirmation by anyone except a superior.

It is plain that this is to be understood of a dignity which requires confirmation by a superior. But the assent of a pope to his election without recourse to a superior is sufficient for confirmation. Hence his withdrawal of consent without recourse to a superior is sufficient for abdication.

11.   Concerning the eternal priesthood of Christ.

The reply is clear from what has been said already. For the priesthood of Christ is eternal because Christ lives to eternity by reason of his self-immolation. I concede

---

[12] James 5.16.
[13] Luke 17.14.

therefore of the pope that his priesthood shall last as long as he lives because he has received the indelible character and will therefore always be a priest, empowered to offer the sacrifice of the altar. But his papal office is not necessarily perpetual throughout his lifetime. A pope can resign or for serious crime be deposed because the papacy is unlike episcopacy and priesthood, being a title of jurisdiction which is changeable and without this jurisdiction a pope is not pope.

Here ends the treatise on royal and papal power written by John of Paris of the order of friars preacher.

INDEX